Odin:
Answer me this eighth question Vafthrudnir,
if you are indeed truly wise;
What is the first thing that you remember
about those earliest of times?

Vafthrudnir:
There were untold winters that existed
before the earth was made
and Bergelmir was born.
My earliest memory is of when
the oldest of giants was placed in a coffin.

Odin:
Answer me this ninth question Vafthrudnir,
if you are indeed truly wise;
Where does the wind come from
that blows over the seas of man?

Vafthrudnir:
There is a giant, disguised as an eagle,
at the furthest edge of the heavens.
He is Hraesvelgr, the corpse swallower.
His huge wings flapping is what makes
the wind that stirs the seas of man.

Odin:
Answer me this tenth question Vafthrudnir,
if you are indeed truly wise;
Why does Niord live among the Aesir?
There are a lot of temples dedicated to him,

but he was not raised among the Aesir.

Vafthrudnir:
The wise leaders of Vanaheim
gave him to the Aesir as a hostage,
but after Ragnarok he'll return
to his home among the Vanir.

Odin:
Answer me this eleventh question Vafthrudnir,
if you are indeed truly wise;
Where do men fight everyday in the courtyards?

Vafthrudnir:
It is the Einherjar, who fight
everyday in Odin's courtyards.
They rush out of the doors to battle
one another every single morning,
but then feast together every evening.

Odin:
Answer me this twelfth question Vafthrudnir,
if you are indeed truly wise;
What are the secrets of the giants and the gods?
Speak truthfully if you are the wisest of giants.

Vafthrudnir:
It's easy to speak truthfully
about those kind of secrets
because I have visited all of the worlds.
I've visited the nine worlds,

and been all the way to Niflheim,
where men go as a last resort.
Odin:
I have travelled far and wide,
and I've undertaken many struggles
as I learned from the greatest of powers,
but this is what I want to know;
Which humans will survive Ragnarok?

Vafthrudnir:
It is Lif and Lifthrasir that will survive.
They'll hide in the branches of Yggdrasil,
and live off the morning dew, before
creating the future generations of man.

Odin:
I have travelled far and wide,
and I've undertaken many struggles,
as I learned from the greatest of powers,
but this is what I want to know;
Where will the new sun come from
after the wolf has destroyed this one?

Vafthrudnir:
The Elfwheel will give birth to a daughter
before she is destroyed by the wolf,
and the daughter will follow
along her mother's well worn path,
when the gods have gone away.

Odin:

I have travelled far and wide,
and I've undertaken many struggles,
as I learned from the greatest of powers,
but this is what I want to know;
Who are the spiritually wise maidens
who so easily find their way across the seas?

Vafthrudnir:
There are three mighty rivers
that flow over the lands
of the maidens who seek their kin.
They are blessed with Hamingja
even though they were raised by giants.

Odin:
I have travelled far and wide,
and I've undertaken many struggles
as I learned from the greatest of powers,
but this is what I want to know;
Which of the Aesir will rule
once Surt's great fire has burned out?

Vafthrudnir:
Vidar and Vali will live
in the shrines of the gods,
after Surt's fire has burned itself out.
Magni and Modi will inherit Miollnir
and continue to do Thor's work.

Odin:
I have travelled far and wide,

and I've undertaken many struggles
as I learned from the greatest of powers,
but this is what I want to know;
What will happen to the elder Odin
when the mighty clash in battle?

Vafthrudnir:
The wolf will devour the Allfather,
but his son Vidar will avenge him,
by ripping the jaws of the wolf apart.

Odin:
I have travelled far and wide,
and I've undertaken many struggles
as I learned from the greatest of powers,
but this is what I want to know;
What did Odin whisper into Balder's ear
before he placed him on the funeral pyre?

Vafthrudnir:
No one knows what you, Odin,
Whispered into the ear of your dead son.
It appears that I've been speaking
with the lips of a dead man
as I spoke of ancient lore,
and the fates of the gods.
I've found myself unknowingly competing
with Odin, the wisest of all beings.

The Havamal

Words from the Allfather, Odin, Himself..
Written for the Modern Heathen

Always look around when you enter a room; you never know where an enemy may be hiding.

A hail to the givers! A guest has arrived. Give him a place to sit. You should hurry to give him a place by the fire.

Fire and warmth are needed for the one who comes in from the cold. Food, drink, and clothing are needed for the man who has traveled over the mountains.

A place to wash up and a warm welcome are needed for the one who comes to the feast. A friendly reception and a chance at conversation.

Wisdom is needed by the one who travels far and wide, anything will pass at home. A man is a joke if he sits with wise men, and yet knows nothing.

No man should brag about how smart he is, a wise man is cautious and silent. When a wise man comes silently to another's home, he will seldom arouse anger; a man's best friend is a store of good sense.

A cautious guest at a feast stays quiet when he hears others whispering. He listens with his ears, and watches with his eyes; so that the wise man can determine what is happening.

Lucky is the man who gains honor and praise for himself. It is difficult to claim what is in another's heart.

Happy is the man who keeps his honor and wisdom while he lives; Bad counsel has often come from other people.

There is no better burden to carry on the road than good sense and manners; it is a great treasure to have when you are in a strange place.

There is no better burden to carry on the road than good sense and manners; and no worse burden to carry than an excess of ale.

Ale is not as good for the sons of man as they say, the more a man drinks the less he is able to think.

The forgetfulness-heron hovers over cups of ale and steals a man's sense; I was bound by that bird's feathers in Gunnlod's court.

I was drunk, I was senselessly drunk in the hall of the wise Fialar; the best bout of drinking ale is when everyone goes home with their sense and reason.

The sons of men should be silent and thoughtful, but bold in battle; a man should be cheerful and generous until he comes to his death.

A coward thinks he will live forever if he stays away from the fight; but old age will not spare him, even if he does avoid the spears.

The fool stares and mumbles to himself when he goes to a feast; but as soon as he drinks, he exposes his thoughts.

The man who travels widely and has experienced a lot knows how each man is ruled, if he is sharp in his wits.

Do not hold onto the horn for long, drink your mead in moderation, speak sensibly or hold your tongue. No man will find fault with you if you go to bed early.

A greedy man who lacks discipline will eat until he becomes sick; a large belly is the butt of jokes among wise men.

Cattle know when to leave the pasture to return home, but the foolish man doesn't know the measure of his own stomach.

The miserable man makes fun of everything; but does not understand that he has faults of his own.

The stupid man stays awake all night and worries about everything; when morning comes, he is tired, and nothing has changed.

The foolish man thinks that everyone who smiles at him is his friend. He doesn't know how they talk about him when he sits with the wise.

The foolish man thinks that everyone who smiles at him is his friend, but when he arrives at the Thing he finds few who will speak up for him.

A foolish man thinks he knows everything as he hides in his own little corner; but he doesn't know what to say when he is confronted by strong men.

A foolish man in the company of his elders should remain silent. No one will know that he doesn't know anything, unless he talks too much. The man who doesn't know anything, doesn't know that he should be quiet.

The man who knows how to ask questions and give answers, seems wise; but the sons of men cannot keep their faults secret.

The man who talks too much will often speak ill-chosen words; a tongue that wags too much will often wag itself into trouble.

Do not make fun of the man who comes to visit your home. Many men seem wise if they aren't asked any questions.

A man thinks he is smart when he leaves the guest who has insulted another; the man who mocks another at the feast table does not know if he is amid enemies.

Many men who are loyal to one another enjoy teasing and arguing with each other at feasts; this could arouse guests to fight amongst each other.

A man should eat early so that he doesn't arrive as a hungry guest, if not then he will sit around staring hungrily and not talking.

It seems like a long journey to visit a bad friend even though he lives close; but the way seems shorter when you travel to a good friend, no matter the distance.

A man should not remain a guest for too long; a welcome guest can wear out that welcome if he stays too late.

A home of your own is always better, because there, you are your own master; two goats and a cheap roof are always better than begging.

A home of your own is always better, because there, you are your own master; a man's heart breaks when he must beg for his meals,

No man should ever take more than a step away from his weapons when he is out; you never know when you may need your spear.

I never found a man who was so generous with his wealth that he would refuse a gift; nor any so rich that he refused a wage that he had earned.

The man who has money does not suffer from need; but saving for those you love could end up in the hands of those you hate; not everything goes as planned.

You should give weapons and clothes to your friends; gifts between friends can cause the relationship to deepen and endure.

To a friend a man should be a friend. Repay a gift with a gift; laughter should be paid with laughter, lies with lies.

To a friend a man should be a friend, to him and to his friend; but do not be a friend to the enemy of your friend.

If you have a friend who you truly trust and wish nothing but good for him, you should mix your blood with his and exchange gifts; go seek him out often.

If there is one, who you don't trust, but who you want nothing but good; speak fairly to him, but think carefully, and repay his treachery with lies.

This is also for the one you don't trust and whose intentions you suspect. Smile when he smiles, choose your words wisely and repay gifts with gifts.

When I was young, I traveled alone and went off the road; I felt like I was rich when I finally met another man, because company is the joy of man.

A man who is generous and brave has the best life; they seldom harbor sorrow. A coward fears many things and the miser worries over every gift he is given.

I gave my clothes to two wooden men in a field; they thought they were champions when they were clothed. A naked man is ashamed.

A fir tree on a hill will wither and die without the protection of its bark and needles; it is the same for a man who has no loved ones, why should he continue to live for a long time?

A peaceful man can love his worthless friend for five days; but on the sixth day, the friendship will die.

A small gift will often buy you praise; with half a loaf of bread and a shared horn of mead, I won a faithful friend.

Small piles of sand, little lakes; some men have small minds; all men are not wise, all men are not alike in wisdom.

A man should be average in wisdom, never too wise; the man who well knows what he knows, he has the best sort of life.

A man should be average in wisdom, never too wise; because an overly wise man is seldom cheerful, especially if he thinks himself all-wise.

A man should be average in wisdom, never too wise; a man is far happier if he doesn't know his fate ahead of time.

Fire is lit by fire, until it is consumed, a flame is kindled by a flame; man becomes clever by speaking with man, but foolish by being silent.

A man should get up early if he plans to take someone else's life or possessions; a sleeping wolf rarely gets his prey, or a sleeping man victory.

The man who has few employees should get up early and get to work; much is lost for the man who sleeps late. Wealth is half-won by activity.

Of dry wood and roofing, a man can know the measure of; likewise, the amount of firewood that will last for a whole winter.

Washed and fed, a man should go to the Thing, even if he is not well dressed; no man should be ashamed of his clothing. Nor of his horse, even if it isn't a good one.

Questions and answers were made with sense by one who would be called wise. Trust only one person with a secret; if three people know, then everyone knows.

He stares and cranes his neck when he wanders the seas, the eagle to the ocean; the same as a man who comes into a crowd and has few friends to speak for him.

A wise man should use his power and authority in moderation; for when he travels with the brave, he will find that no one is the boldest of all.

For every word that one man says to another; he will often get paid back for it.

To some places I came too early, to others I arrived too late; the ale was already drunk, or not yet brewed; the unpopular man seldom shows up at the right moment.

Here and there I might have been invited when I had no need of food; or two hams would be hanging in a trusted friend's home when I'd already eaten one.

Fire is best among the sons of men, as is the sight of the sun; just like the gift of health, if a man can live without vice.

No man lacks everything, even if his health is bad, one may be blessed with sons, another with kinsmen, one may have wealth, and another may be rich in good deeds.

It is better to live than to be dead, the living man will get the cow. I saw the fire die out in a rich man's house while death stood at his door.

A lame man can ride a horse, a handless man can herd cattle, a deaf man can fight; it is better to be a blind man, than to burn on a funeral pyre. No one needs a corpse.

A son is good to have, even if he is born after the father has died. Memorial stones are seldom raised by anyone other than kinsmen.

These two are often enemies, the tongue is the slayer of the head; I expect to find a clenched first hidden under every fur cloak.

Night is easily awaited when you know that you have enough to eat; short are a ship's yards, an autumn night can change quickly, the weather can change a lot in five days, and more over the course of a month.

The man who knows nothing does not know that many are fools to others; one man may be rich and another poor. He should not be blamed for this.

Cattle die; kinsmen die; you yourself will also die, but the glory of honor never dies for the man who has earned a good name.

Cattle die; kinsmen die; you yourself will also die; One thing I know that never dies is the reputation of a dead man.

Fully stocked cabinets I saw at the rich man's sons; now they carry a beggar's staff; wealth is like the wink of an eye; it is the most unreliable of friends.

When a foolish man gets money or the love of a good woman, his pride grows, but not his common sense; he walks in a fool's blindness.

It is known, when you ask the runes of divine origin which the great gods made and were colored by the bond of secret wisdom, it is best for you to remain silent.

The day should be praised after the sun has set on it, a woman after she has been placed on her funeral pyre, a sword's edge after it has been tested, the girl after she has been married, the ice after you have crossed it, the ale after it has been drank.

A good time to cut down a tree is when the wind blows, rowing on the sea is best when done in fine weather, the darkness is made for talking to a girl, the day has many eyes; you need speed from a ship, protections from a shield, strength from a sword, and kisses from a girl.

You should drink ale by the fire, slide over ice on skates, buy a horse when it is lean, and a blade when it is rusty. You can fatten up a horse and train a dog.

You should not trust the words of a girl, nor what a woman says; their hearts were created on a whirling wheel and fickleness is fixed in their hearts.

Do not trust a breaking bow, a flaring flame, a growling wolf, a cawing crow, a bellowing boar, a rootless tree, a rising wave, a boiling kettle,

A flying arrow, a breaking wave, one-night old ice, a coiled serpent, the bed talk of a woman, a broken sword, a playful bear, or a king's child,

A sick calf, a stubborn slave, a prophet who has nothing but fair words, a newly killed dead man,

No man should trust in a newly sown field, nor too soon on a son; the weather rules the field and brains the son, both are risky.

A brother's killer, even if met on a wide road, a house half-burned, a horse that is as fast as the wind, (the mount is useless with a broken leg). No man should be so confident that he trusts in these.

So is the love of women, who have false hearts; it's like riding a horse over slippery ice without spiked shoes, a frisky two year old that is badly trained, or like sailing in a violent storm with a rudderless ship, or like a lame man chasing a reindeer across slippery rocks.

I can speak openly for I have known both; how treacherous a man's heart can be towards women; when we speak most fairly, then we think most falsely, this traps even the most cunning.

You should speak fair and offer precious gifts if you desire a woman's love; praise the beauty of a woman; he who flatters will get his wish.

No man should ever blame another for being in love; often a wise man is beguiled by a pretty face, when the foolish man is not.

Nor shall one-man reproach another for what is common among men; wise men are often turned into fools by overwhelming desire.

The mind alone knows what lies near the heart, it alone sees into the depths of the soul; no sickness is worse for a wise man than not to find contentment in anything.

This I learned while I hid in the reeds and waited for my love; my body and my soul she meant to me, yet I did not win her.

Billing's girl I found asleep on the bed; she was as radiant as the sun; no princely treasure seemed as great as to live with her beauty.

"Toward evening, Odin, you should return if you want to win the maid; all will be lost if we don't keep this a secret between us."

Back I ran and thought myself lucky; this I thought: that I would have her tender touch and pleasure.

When I returned though, all the gallant warriors were wide awake, with blazing torches and barricades, the path was made dangerous for me.

When I returned near dawn, the warriors were asleep, but I found a vicious dog tied to the bed of the beautiful woman.

Many a sweet maid, when you get to know her, is fickle of heart when it comes to men; I found that out when I tried to seduce that wise woman; every hurdle that clever girl devised for me and I ended up with nothing at all.

A man in his own home should be cheerful and merry with his guests, he should be shrewd about himself, with a good memory and easy speech, if he wants to be wise; an idiot the man is called who can't say much for himself that is the hallmark of a fool.

I visited the old giant, now I have returned; I did not gain much there because of my silence; with many words I won success in Suttung's Halls.

Gunlord sat on her golden throne and gave me a drink of the precious mead; a poor reward I gave her in return.

With Rati the auger I made room for myself and gnawed through the rock; over and under me went the giant's road, thus I risked my head.

A well-earned drink I made good use of; the wise lack for little; for Odrerir has come up to the sanctuaries of me.

I doubt I would have escaped from the giant's dwelling, if I had not used Gunnlod, that good woman, and put my arms around her.

The next day the frost giants went to hear Odin's advice in his high hall; they asked about Bolverk; whether he was among the gods; or whether Suttung had vanquished him.

I think Odin swore an oath on a sacred ring, how can his pledge be trusted? He left Suttung without his mead, and Gunnlod in tears!

It is time to speak from the wise one's seat, by the well of Urd; I saw and was silent, I watched and I thought, I listened to what men said; I heard them discussing runes, there was no lack of knowledge in the High One's hall, in the High One's hall, I heard them say.

I suggest you take this advice: It will be useful if you learn it, it will serve you well if you have it: don't get up at night, unless you are on guard duty, or if you have to use the bathroom.

I suggest you take this advice: It will be useful if you learn it, it will serve you well if you have it: Never fall asleep with a witch so that she encloses you with her arms.

She will make it so that you don't care about the Thing or your duties; you won't want food or the company of your friends, you will fall asleep full of sadness.

I suggest you take this advice: It will be useful if you learn it, it will serve you well if you have it: Never have another man's wife as a close confidant.

I suggest you take this advice: It will be useful if you learn it, it will serve you well if you have it: If you are traveling over a mountain or across a fjord, make sure you are carrying enough food.

I suggest you take this advice: It will be useful if you learn it, it will serve you well if you have it: Never let an evil man know your suffering; from a wicked man you will never get a good thought in return for your trust.

I saw a man hurt by the words of a terrible woman; her poisonous tongue brought about his death without a shred of proof.

I suggest you take this advice: It will be useful if you learn it, it will serve you well if you have it: If you have a friend that you trust, go to visit him often; stickers and weeds grow thick on the roads that are not traveled.

I suggest you take this advice: It will be useful if you learn it, it will serve you well if you have it: Draw good natured men to you in friendship and learn helpful charms all your life.

I suggest you take this advice: It will be useful if you learn it, it will serve you well if you have it: Do not be the first one to end a friendship; sorrow will eat at your heart if you don't have someone to share your thoughts with.

I suggest you take this advice: It will be useful if you learn it, it will serve you well if you have it: You should never argue with an idiot.

Because you will never get a fair return from a man with bad intentions; but a good man will reassure you with his words.

That is the true meaning of friendship, when a man can share all his thoughts; anything is better than someone who is fickle; you do not have a true friend if he only tells you pleasant things.

I suggest you take this advice: It will be useful if you learn it, it will serve you well if you have it: you should not exchange angry words with an inferior person; the better man often retreats when the lesser man fights.

I suggest you take this advice: It will be useful if you learn it, it will serve you well if you have it: Make your own shoes and the shaft for your spear. A shoe can be made to fit wrong and a spear shaft can be warped if the maker wishes you harm

I suggest you take this advice: It will be useful if you learn it, it will serve you well if you have it: when you meet evil then call it evil, and give your enemy no peace.

I suggest you take this advice: It will be useful if you learn it, it will serve you well if you have it: Never be gladdened by wickedness but take pleasure in good things.

I suggest you take this advice: It will be useful if you learn it, it will serve you well if you have it: Never stare up at the sky during a battle -- the sons of men can go crazy -- and others may try to entrap you.

I suggest you take this advice: It will be useful if you learn it, it will serve you well if you have it: if you want to talk a good woman into having a secret love affair with you, make good promises to her and keep them: No man will tire of a good thing.

I suggest you take this advice: It will be useful if you learn it, it will serve you well if you have it: I tell you to be careful but not too careful; be cautious of ale and of another man's wife and thirdly, be wary of thieves.

I suggest you take this advice: It will be useful if you learn it, it will serve you well if you have it: never snub or make fun of a guest or a traveler.

Often, the ones already seated inside do not know who the newcomers are related to; no man is so good that he is without flaws, or so bad that he is worth nothing.

I suggest you take this advice: It will be useful if you learn it, it will serve you well if you have it: Never laugh at an elderly wise man! Often what the old one says is good; wrinkled lips often speak wise words.

I suggest you take this advice: It will be useful if you learn it, it will serve you well if you have it: do not abuse your guests or drive them from your home, and treat the poor with kindness!

It takes strength to open your door for everyone; be generous so that no one wishes you ill.

I suggest you take this advice: It will be useful if you learn it, it will serve you well if you have it: When you drink ale, seek out the power of the Earth, because Earth soaks up drunkenness the way fire works against sickness, oak works as a laxative, and an ear of corn against witchcraft, the home works against household strife, for hatred you should call upon the moon, earthworms for swelling, and runes work against evil; a field of dirt must soak up a flood.

I know that I hung on a windswept tree for nine long nights, wounded with a spear and dedicated to Odin, myself to myself, on that tree of which no man knows from where its roots came from.

They gave me no bread to eat, and offered no drink from a horn, I peered downward and searched the depths; I took up the runes, screaming I took them, then I fell back.

I learned nine powerful spells from the famous son of Bolthor, Bestla's father and I got a drink of the precious mead of inspiration, I drained Odrerir, the kettle that contained it.
I began to thrive and to grow wiser, and to grow greater and to prosper; for me, one word grew from one word and then found a new word for me, one deed grew from one deed and then found a new deed for me.

You must find the runes and great letters, very great letters, very stiff letters, which the great sage colored, and the mighty powers made and the runemaster to the gods carved.

Odin among the Aesir,   Dain among the elves,   Dvalin among the dwarfs, Asvid among the giants.

Do you know how to carve them?
Do you know how to interpret them?
Do you know how to color them?
Do you know how to question them?
Do you know how to pray to them?
Do you know how to transmit them?
Do you know how to destroy them?

It is better to not pray, than to sacrifice too much; one gift always calls for another one; it is better to send nothing, than to slaughter too much.

I know the spells which a queen doesn't know, nor do the sons of men; "help" one is called, and it will aid you against legal problems, and sorrows, and all kinds of anxiety.

I know a second one which should be known to those who want to be doctors.

I know a third one that can be useful when you are in great need, it can shackle the feet of your enemies; I can make their blades dull so that their weapons can't harm you.

I know a fourth one that I can use if my enemies bind my limbs; I can chant a charm that will set me free, the shackles will spring from my feet, and the chains will fall off my hands.

I know a fifth one that can be useful if I see an arrow soaring toward my army; if I can see it flying through the air, then I can stop it in mid-flight.

I know a sixth one that can be used if a man poisons me: and if someone tries to use magic to harm me, then it will turn and harm him, not me.

I know a seventh one that can be used to combat a raging fire: it can never get so big that I can't put it out; I know what to chant.

I know an eighth one which everyone should learn; when hate flares up between the sons of fellow warriors, I can quickly bring it to a peaceful end.

I know a ninth one that I can use when I need to save my ship; I can calm the fiercest wind and lull the stormiest sea to sleep.

I know a tenth one that I can use if I see witches flying through the air; I can cause them to wander far away from their bodies as well as their minds.

I know an eleventh one that will help me lead my loyal friends into battle; below the shields I chant the charm, and they will move forward with confidence, safely into battle, safely away from battle, safely they will return from everywhere.

I know a twelfth one which I can use if I find a corpse hanging in a tree with a noose around its neck: I can carve and color runes so that the man can walk and talk with me.

I know a thirteenth one that if I pour water over a young warrior, he will not be killed when he goes into battle, no weapon will be able to strike him down.

I know a fourteenth one that will help me name the gods in front of a group of warriors: of the Aesir and the elves, I know every detail, only the very wise can say that.

I know a fifteenth one which the dwarf Thiodrerir invoked before Delling's doors: He called for power to be given to the Aesir and advancement for the elves, and a thoughtful mind for the mightiest of the gods.

I know a sixteenth one that I can use if I want all of a woman's heart and love: I can turn the thoughts of a pale beauty and change her mind completely.

I know a seventeenth one that will keep any young woman from wanting to reject me. You will want these spells for a long time; they will be useful to you if you learn them, they will serve you well if you have them.

I know an eighteenth one which I will never teach to a girl, or to another man's wife – it is always better if only one person knows what follows the end of a spell – except that one woman who embraces me, or the one who is my sister.

Now the High One's song has been sung in the High One's hall: It is very useful to the sons of men, and useless to the sons of giants, good luck to the one who sang, good luck to the one who understood! The ones who learn it will benefit. Good luck to those who listened.

The Nine Noble Virtues
Six Fold Goals
Five Further Thews

As humans, we often look for a guide or a manual on how to live our lives on a daily basis. We look for a moral compass to derive value from and to steer our decisions, actions and choices. As Heathens we have been given the Nine Noble Virtues, Six Fold Goals, and Five Further Thews. The information in each is meant to guide our behavior and give us the moral and ethical standards that have been drawn from a number of sources, both historic and literary. Such sources include the Havamal, the Eddas and other Icelandic Sagas. One unique thing about Heathenism is that we get to decide the meaning of the writings for ourselves and how to apply it in our daily lives.

The Nine Noble Virtues

- 🐗 Courage
- 🐗 Truth
- 🐗 Honor
- 🐗 Fidelity
- 🐗 Discipline
- 🐗 Hospitality
- 🐗 Industriousness
- 🐗 Self –Reliance
- 🐗 Perseverance

The Nine Noble Virtues come right out of the Havamal, which is Old Norse for "The Words of the High One." The passages all deal with Odin and have him giving out advice about life, or instructions on moral conduct.

The following virtues are taken directly from those passages. These are ideals that our ancestors knew very well. They followed these principles and adhered to the lessons, and in turn taught them to their children in the form of stories. It has been my experience that by integrating these concepts into our daily life, you will live an easier, yet a more noble life.

❖ The shortest and surest way to live with honor in the world is to be in reality what we would appear to be; all human virtues increase and strengthen themselves by the practice and experience of them. –Socrates

Courage

This is the ability to do something even though it frightens you. To do something no matter how difficult or dangerous it is. To face pain and grief yet endure and carry on with that loss.

Our ancestors were known for their courage and bravery in battle, but courage encompasses far more than simply being brave in battle.

It takes courage to have a set of beliefs that you are unwilling to compromise. To live by a code of ethics and to stand up against those who want you to surrender your beliefs in favor of theirs.

There is a reason that courage comes first in the list of these virtues. It's because it takes courage to follow and live up to each and every one. Courage is needed in every aspect of your life. Whether male or female, and no matter the role you choose to play in life.

In today's society where conformism and political correctness rule, it is more important than ever to have the courage to cling to your beliefs as an onslaught of negativity attempts to make you kneel to the masses.

❖ The test of courage comes when we are in the minority. – Emerson

- The brave and generous have the best lives. They're seldom sorry. --The Havamal
- A coward thinks he will live forever if he stays away from the fight; but old age will not spare him, even if he does avoid the spears. – The Havamal

Truth

Truth is the state of being in accordance with fact and reality. It is sincerity in action, character, and utterance. It means having the quality of being free from pretense, deceit, or hypocrisy. Simply put – don't lie; to yourself or others. Lying is an act of cowardice, if you are lying for or to yourself. If you live according to what you believe in your heart, you'll have no reason to be deceitful about your actions. If you do not think an action is right, then don't do it. If something isn't true, then don't say it. Be confident in your words and actions.

With that being said, some people may perceive a situation or action differently that you do. Truth does not require you to assert your perspective on everyone that sees it differently. You should be respectful of another's view and whatever beliefs that they wish to live by. This is about your truth, your honesty.

A true Heathen should make truth a part of his or her life. But like courage, and every other virtue, it shouldn't be used stupidly. You should never compromise your life or give your enemy power over you. In the

Havamal, Odin advises, "If there is one, who you don't trust, but who you want nothing but good; speak fairly to him, but think carefully, and repay his treachery with lies." Not every situation will be black and white, be truthful to yourself about that too.

- ❖ There is always a way to be honest without being brutal. -- Author Dobrin
- ❖ There should be truth in thought, truth in speech, and truth in action. –Gandhi
- ❖ When you meet evil then call it evil, and give your enemy no peace. – The Havamal

Honor

A keen sense of ethical conduct which allows one to be regarded with great respect and esteem. A quality of worthiness and respectability that affects one's social standing amongst their family, neighborhoods, and society as a whole. Without a sense of honor, you can never feel like a completely noble human being.

Honor is not the easiest concept to define because it is not a black and white character trait. You may be able to define it as your internal integrity or dignity. Your personal honor and value is determined by your internal beliefs, and the ethics that you wish to live up to. Your tribal honor and value is determined by your family or societal group.

Of course, there is a difference between personal honor, and tribal honor. One is the sense of worth that comes from within yourself while the other is more closely akin to reputation. The difference is that honor is when you feel pride at what you have done, even if no one else noticed or cared. Your reputation comes as an acknowledgment of perceived good actions, even if done by accident, and in which you take no pride in. It is your intentions and your actions which determine your honor, not necessarily what other people may think. Although one can definitely be a reflection of the other.

A person who lives according to a code of honor will have few regrets in life. He will know that he has done the best that he could to live up to the standards that he believes in.

- ❖ Honor is a harder master than the law. --Mark Twain
- ❖ Our own heart, and not other men's opinion, form our true honor. --Samuel Coleridge
- ❖ The glory of honor never dies for the man who has earned a good name. – The Havamal

Fidelity

To be faithful to a person, cause or belief which is demonstrated by continual loyalty and support. To never turn one's back and remain undivided. The concept of fidelity also means to remain true or loyal to the oaths that you give. Oaths were extremely important to Viking age Heathens, as it is to the gods.

The name of our religion means "True to the Aesir." True in this concept means loyal, the very name of our religion gives emphasis to how important fidelity is. We even have a goddess who hears all oaths and punishes the perjurers while rewarding those who keep their oaths. Her name is Var.

Without fidelity there can be no strong commitments or unions. Fidelity breeds trust, and trust strengthens bonds. Bonds to your gods, your family, your friends and your spouse.

A strong sense of fidelity lends itself to the concept of courage, and gives you strength when you know that you do not stand alone. Give oaths to those who are worthy and encourage others to do the same.

- ❖ To a friend a man should be a friend, to him and to his friends; but do not be a friend to the enemy of your friend. – The Havamal
- ❖ If you have a friend who you truly trust and wish nothing but good for him, you should mix your blood with his and exchange gifts; go seek him out often. – The Havamal
- ❖ Be slow to give your friendship, but when you have given it, strive to make it lasting. –Isocrates

Discipline

The suppression of desire to pursue something greater. Using reason to determine the best course of action, regardless of their own personal desires, which may be contrary to what must take place. To stay the course and having the resolve to continue doing what must be done. It takes discipline to accomplish anything of value: whether that is getting good grades, advancing in your career, building a better physique, or following nine noble virtues. It all takes a conscious effort to achieve, and that is exactly what discipline is. It is the resolve to accomplish some act, and the strength to resist the impulses that will interfere or keep you from reaching your goal.

You must have discipline to live according to your own personal code, rather than according to what politicians or cultural dictators say. This means taking responsibility for your actions and practicing restraint. There are times when things that are legal may go against your code of honor, and there are many things that a government may declare as illegal that is permitted within your personal standards. In order to stay true to what you believe in, you need to practice self-discipline. Especially if you hope to have control over your own self-worth. It takes discipline to achieve success, whether that is as an individual or as a larger group. To have discipline is to have focus.

- He who lives without discipline dies without honor. -- Icelandic Proverb
- What lies in our power to do, it lies in our power not to do. –Aristotle
- A greedy man who lacks discipline will eat until he becomes sick; a large belly is the butt of jokes among wise men. – The Havamal

Hospitality

This is the relationship between a guest and a host, wherein the host receives the guest with goodwill. This includes the reception and entertainment of guests, visitors, or strangers. The concept of hospitality extends past the providing of food and shelter; it includes making sure that they do not come to harm while under their roof.

The Vikings believed that the gods would show up and visit Midgard in human form, at any given time. They believed you could never be sure who your guests were and they didn't want to inadvertently disrespect or offend a god in disguise.

This is not the reason that a Heathen treats everyone with respect and courtesy but it is a cautious warning. A Heathen does this because it is part of our code of ethics. We treat others with hospitality, not because they deserve it, but because that is how we behave toward others. It is about our own principles, not about what others may deserve.

- A place to wash up and a warm welcome are needed for the one who comes to the feast. – The Havamal
- Do not abuse your guests or drive them from your home, and treat the poor with kindness. – The Havamal

Industriousness

The way of working energetically and devotedly to complete a task or one of life's daily toils in a hard-working and diligent manner. Not being lazy, but having great care and attention in the steadfast application of one's work and effort.

Remember the old saying: "If something is worth doing, then it's worth doing well." Do everything with pride and to the best of your ability. The gods and our ancestors looked down on those who were lazy. A person needs to work hard and smart to take care of his family, and to achieve success.

This does not apply only to your career, but to everything that you do; your entire way of life. A Heathen is a person who strives for excellence. He or she will do everything to the highest standard that they can reach. We set high expectations for ourselves in everything we can do, and we refuse to lower those standards in our work, or in our personal beliefs.

- Hold yourself responsible for a higher standard than anybody else expects of you. Never excuse yourself. -- Henry Ward Beecher
- The man who has few employees should get up early and get to work; much is lost for the man who sleeps late. Wealth is half-won by activity. – The Havamal
- A man should get up early if he plans to take someone else's life or possessions; a sleeping wolf rarely gets his prey, or a sleeping man victory. – The Havamal

Self-Reliance

The state of reliance on oneself or one's own powers and resources by not requiring any aid, support or interaction from others for survival. A state of personal independence.

As a people we are by nature independent beings. This doesn't mean we don't need other people or enjoy being with others and socializing, but rather that we strive to ensure that we don't have to depend on others for survival. A Heathen is responsible for taking care of themselves and their families; this is their first and foremost responsibility and duty. One can never be truly comfortable if their family's welfare depends on something outside of their control.

Being dependant on someone else for your needs puts you at a dangerous disadvantage. Such a position can make it very hard for you to choose between your principles and your livelihood. Always depend upon yourself for your own sense of self-worth. Self-reliance means to be self-sufficient, to rely on yourself as much as it is possible to do so. Strive to be as independent of outside influences whenever possible.

- ❖ The greatest fruit of self-sufficiency is freedom. -- Epicurus
- ❖ It is thrifty to prepare today for the wants of tomorrow. – Aesop
- ❖ Make your own shoes and the shaft for your spear. A shoe can be made to fit wrong and a spear shaft can be warped if the maker wishes you harm. – The Havamal
- ❖ A home of your own is always better, because there you are your own master; a man's heart breaks when he must beg for his meals. – The Havamal

Perseverance

To continue forward no matter the obstacles, to always strive to better one's circumstances. This comes from the Havamal: "I began to thrive and grow wiser, and to grow greater and to prosper; for me, one word grew from one word and then found a new word for me, one deed grew from one deed and then found a new deed for me." That is the way you persevere, one word then the next. One deed, then another. One step will lead to the next. No matter the hurdles that you have to overcome, you have to climb them one at a time. Focus on the end goal, and move toward it. One step will lead to the next step, and then find one more.

Ignore the ones who say that you can't do it. They have no concept of what it means to succeed, or to have a moral code that demands that you not quit. Always strive for improvement. Never give up or surrender, especially in the face of adversity. Try and try again, until you get it done.

You don't try to be a Heathen – you either are or you are not. You either have honor and integrity or you don't. For the Heathen, falling short does not mean failing, it means learning, and being determined to do better next time.

- ❖ First say to yourself what you would be; and then do what you have to do. --Epictetus
- ❖ There is nothing impossible to him who will try. --Alexander the Great
- ❖ It is better to fight and fail than to live without hope. – Volsung Saga

Six-Fold Goals

Virtues are something you live up to, while goals are something to be achieved. They are not directions for you to live by; they are to be reached for. These are not achievements you reach down and pick up off the ground; they require effort, fortitude and dedication. You may not reach the pinnacle of each. The point is to improve yourself and make improvements within your life, moving step by step toward each goal. Each step taken toward a goal is a success; every struggle you overcome is a victory. Every victory, every step forward brings joy and accomplishment. The gods embody these goals; their actions are set down in stories as examples for us to imitate.

- Right
- Wisdom
- Might
- Harvest
- Frith
- Love

Right is the quality to do what is correct, just, proper or honorable. These qualities are best embodied by both Tyr and Forseti. To do right it is sometimes necessary to set aside personal preferences, prejudices, and desires.

Not an easy task, but that is exactly why they are goals that you have to work toward.

Forseti is the god of justice and righteousness. It is said that he will patiently listen to each side and then will reach a judgment that is so fair that none can find fault with his decision.

Tyr represents a different form of right. When the gods went to bind the vicious and dangerous wolf, Fenris, they had to trick him. They had a thin chord made and challenged Fenris to let them bind him to test his strength. The wolf demanded that a hand be placed in his mouth before he'd accept the challenge. Tyr didn't hesitate to offer up his sword hand in what became an honorable sacrifice. He did what was right for Asgard and the wolf will remain bound till Ragnarok.

Forseti is right because he is correct and just. Tyr is right because he is proper and honorable. Both are worthy goals to work toward.

Wisdom is the ability to utilize the knowledge that you have obtained in a productive and beneficial manner. The more knowledge that you acquire the wiser and more informed your decision will be. Odin challenged himself to learn more and more so that he could become wiser. He sacrificed an eye to drink from Mimir's well of wisdom and put himself through various trials to gather knowledge and hone his wit. Odin believes that wisdom can only be obtained by collecting knowledge and through experience.

Knowledge and learning come from the sacrifice of your time and effort, but then you must throw yourself into the maelstrom of life to form that knowledge into wisdom. You do not need to sacrifice an eye or hang from a tree for nine days and nights without food or water, but that is the value that Odin puts on knowledge and wisdom. Struggles are only obstacles for you to learn from as you move forward in your evolution. Tripping is not a failure it is wisdom gained from pain. You become wiser when you recognize your mistakes and stop blaming others for your circumstances.

Might can be best expressed as the powers, authority, resources, and physical strength of an individual or group. Might is a version of independence because it allows you to live an autonomous life uncontrolled by another human being.

Thor represents might in a variety of ways. He has the power of Miollnir, the physical strength of his musculature, the resources of regenerating goats and the authority of someone who is in charge of their own home. Physical strength comes from exercise and dedication, in turn makes you healthier and gives you a more robust physique. You will live longer and have a better quality of life. You will be more capable of defending yourself and your loved ones. A healthier and more powerful physique will also elevate you in other people's eyes. They will understand that it takes commitment, resolve, and dedication to improve yourself. Your confidence will increase which will in turn give you access to resources that will increase your power and authority. Everyone respects a goal orientated hard worker, and exercise is a physical demonstration of how hard you can work.

Every goal, no matter how great or small, takes steps. Every step will lead you to another, but they are steps on a staircase, and a set of stairs will take you higher; a little closer to the goals that will improve your life.

Harvest is about reaping the rewards for the crops that you have planted and for the work you have put in. Too many people labor and toil away at an activity only to have someone else harvest the benefits of their hard work. This goal is about planning and pursing the end result of that plan. Think about the harvest, but first think about the necessary steps that you need to take to create a garden. You need to prepare the soil, you need to pull the weeds, till it, fertilize it, then plow, and finally you get to plant your seeds. After you have planted your crop, you need to water it, protect it, and you need to nurture your crop as it matures. Finally, after all of those steps, hard work and time, you get to harvest your crop.

Whether you are harvesting an actual physical crop or whether you are harvesting the result of careful planning and hard work; the steps are the same. You must first decide on what kind of crop you want to harvest. Do you want more money? A promotion? The pretty woman across the way? A healthier relationship with your significant other? A better physique? How do you get there? Where do your seeds need to be planted, and then how do you go about nurturing those seeds?

Harvest is about taking initiative, making plans, working hard and then reaping the rewards of what you have earned. Frey is the god of fertility and fertility is about production, and then harvesting the crops that you have planted.

Frith is the peaceful reflection that Frigga embodies as goddess of the home, childbirth, and marriage; all things that symbolize stability and joy. The goddess invites husbands and wives who are especially committed to one another into her palace so that they never have to be separated again. An example of eternal joy, calm and peace. Frith is that feeling you get when you return home after a long absence. It is sanctuary; that absence of chaos and stress that allows you to embrace a peaceful and tranquil calm.

Frith is a true statement of peace, it is that lull between struggles that allows you to shrug off one weight before picking up the next one. The ability to embrace frith, particularly inner frith, requires practice and effort. Frigga's calm represents that inner peace that she displays as she moves forward from one challenge to the next. A state of frith allows you to remain calm in the face of adversity. It is a goal because it takes effort and dedication to learn and develop the ability to embrace that moment of calm as it comes, and then retain it as you face the outer turmoil to come.

Love in this context is the thrill of living and joy of play. This is the unbridled desire to experience different aspects of life. This is that adventurous spirit that pushes us to conquer different activities and pulls us up and out of those comfort zones. Too many of us ignore the zeal of life and become stagnant, lazy and lackluster reflections of our childhood selves. We age, mature, and lose our desire for exploration and excitement. We lose our love of life and become mired down with the ideals of materialism.

The gods and goddesses have Idunna and her golden apples to keep them young and full of the love for life. For the sons and daughters of man; we must make love a goal and constantly reach out to grab it. Freyja leads the way when it comes to love; whether she is inspiring physical satisfactions of lust; or that human need to play and explore. She represents that invigorating spirit that inspires all of nature to renew itself. Love of life is like a fire, the flames must be fanned; the fire needs to be fed. The goal here is one of constant motion. Love is zest for life. It is bright and glorious. Make love your goal; feed your fire with experiences and challenges that will pull you forward.

Five Further Thews

- 🐗 Openhandedness
- 🐗 Evenheadedness
- 🐗 Strength
- 🐗 Wisdom
- 🐗 Kinship

An additional set of values that work with and enhance the Nine Noble Virtues. They are here to reinforce the concepts of a heathen lifestyle. The word "Thews" means strengths, so the literal interpretation is Five Additional Strengths.

- **Openhandedness** – The giving or sharing of one's abundance without hesitation. The quality of being generous with the excess that you have. Not what you need to survive, but what you have extra of, and hence can live without.

- **Evenheadedness** – The ability to remain calm and rational in any given situation. The ability to reach a decision in a fair, honest and unbiased fashion. To give all sides careful consideration before coming to a conclusion.

- **Strength** – The ability to endure the hardships that life will inevitably throw your way. This is the ability that allows you to get back up after being knocked down. This allows you to overcome any obstacle and continue to move forward to reach your goals.

- **Wisdom** -- To have true wisdom you must accumulate knowledge and then develop the ability to use it in a constructive and meaningful manner.

- **Kinship** – Family. Loyalty to a close knit community that has the same values that you have. A group of people that can rely upon when you are needed, and give you the resources to rely on when you are in need. A mutually beneficial relationship.

REDE OF HONOR

1. In all you do consider its benefit or harm upon yourself, your children, and your people.

2. All that which you do will return to you, sooner or later, for good or ill. Thus, strive always to do good to others, or at least strive always to be just.

3. Be honest with yourself and others. This above all "*To thine own self be true*".

4. Humankind, and especially your own family and folk, has the spark of divinity within it. Protect and nurture that spark.

5. Give your word sparingly and adhere to it like iron.

6. In the world your first trust and responsibility should be to your own people yet be kind and proper to others whenever possible.

7. What you have, hold!

8. Pass on to others only those words that you have personally verified.

9. Be honest with others and let them know that you expect honesty in return always.

10. The fury of the moment plays folly with the truth, to keep one's head is a virtue.

11. Know which battles should be fought and which battles should be avoided. Also know when to break off a conflict. For there are times when the minions of chaos are simply too strong or when fate is absolutely unavoidable.

12. When you gain power use it carefully and use it well

13. Courage and honor endure forever; their echoes remain when the mountains have crumbled to dust.

14. Pledge friendship and your services to those who are worthy, strengthen those of your people and they will strengthen you.

15. Love and care for your family and have the fierceness of a wolf in their protection.

16. Honor yourself, have self-pride, do your best & forgive yourself when you must.

17. Try always to be above reproach in the eyes of the world.

18. Those of our people should always endeavor to settle any differences among themselves peaceably and quietly.

19. The laws of the land should always be obeyed whenever possible and within reason. For in the main they have been chosen with wisdom.

20. Have pride in yourself, your family, and your folk. They are your promise for the future.

21. Do not neglect your mate and children.

22. Every one of our people should work according to the best that he can do, no matter how small or how great. We are all in this world together, thus we must always help each other along.

23. One advances individually and collectively only by working in harmony with the natural order of the world.

24. The seeking of wisdom is a high virtue, love of truth, honor, courage and loyalty are the hallmark of a noble soul.

25. Be prepared for whatever the future brings.

26. Life with all its joys, struggles and ambiguities is to be embraced and lived to the fullest.

The Way of the Einherjar

Hung I was on the windswept tree. Nine full nights I hung, pierced by a spear, a pledge to the god, To Odin, myself to myself, on that tree, which none can know the source, from whence its root has run.

None gave me bread; none brought a horn. Then low to earth I looked. I caught up the runes, roaring I took them, And fainting, back I fell.

Nine mighty lays I learned from the son of Bolthorn, Bestla's father, And a draught I had of the holy mead poured out of Ordrerir.

Then fruitful I grew, and greatly to thrive, In wisdom began to wax. A single word to a second word led, A single poem a second found.
   –Odin's Song Havamal
   Stanzas 138 – 141
   (Emphasis added)

Trustworthiness
By Brodgar

What determines trustworthiness? Loyalty and honesty determine a person's trustworthiness. Through loyalty we learn to respect others, to defend honor and to value the bonds we share with friends and kinsmen. Honesty is the quality of being in agreement with reality or the facts "that which is" or "that which exists."

Our Ancestors considered honesty or what they call sooth to be one of the hallmarks of noble men and women, since liars were often viewed as lowly and vile. Liars and those who utter falsehoods (slander) about others in line with bearers, wade through the river Vadgelmir in horrible pain. "A heavy doom is dealt to men who in Vathgelmir's waters wade; he who untruth utters and on others lies, long will he linger there."--Reginsmal

This river is made from the venom of the serpents, whose whittled back forms the hall in Nastrond. As they wade, Hels/Urds ravens repeatedly pluck their eyes of their heads, which grow back to they can continue this. In an honor-based society such as the one in early Northern Europe lying about someone was serious business. Known as "honor-robbers" they could bring about much harm to those they disgraced. As bad as it is to commit a crime it is much worse to be accused of one you are innocent of by garrulous tongue. "A man I saw sorely besotted through a wicked woman's words, her baleful tongue did work his lane, through good and unguilty he was." – Havamal Stanza 118.

The role of slander is one in which Loki is particular vested in, possibly furthering the conclusion that Vadgelmir is the stream of venom since he is punished by poison of the serpent. The plucking of the eyes might simply be a practical idea; one cannot speak of that which they do not see. "With his friend a man should be friends
ever and play back gift for gift, laughter for laughter, he learns to give and eke leasing for lies." – Havamal Stanza 42.

Still a man must be able to defend himself from the cunning wiles of those with deceptive hearts, which is why men can exchange "a lie for a lie," as part of the orlog concept. To be honest both and to yourself is to accept things as they are, which is one of the trust necessary for the interaction between individual human beings. It weakens us to lie, it weakens our integrity and stems from a fear to face reality, to face the truth. In essence, most lies are either told out of fear or malevolence, protecting us from whatever it is we feel we cannot deal with.

It takes strength and integrity to be loyal, for sometimes you might be called upon to make unpopular decisions that happen to be the right ones. Through loyalty we learn to respect others, to defend honor and to value the bonds we share with friends and kinsmen.

Wyrd/Orlog

For Heathen peoples, Wyrd was the main force that determined the course of events in the universe. Much of what happened didn't happen because of random chance, but instead because it was fated to happen. Almost all beings were subject to fate; even the gods themselves. For all the power that the gods possess, the power of the Norns is even greater.

The Norns are a trio of female entities whose abilities are unmatched by any other beings. They exist at the base of Yggdrasil, beneath one of its mighty roots. There they weave the Web of Wyrd for all the inhabitants of the cosmos, cutting the last strand at the end of the person's life.

The three Norns are Urd, Verdandi, and Skuld. Their names are derived from various forms of the verb "to be." The first Norn is connected with the "Ur," or primal nature of a thing, the part of the past that shapes what will come. Verdandi makes up the "becoming" aspect of the trio, the constantly changing present. Skuld is that which will be a reaction to what has gone before.

A loose interpretation has led many to believe that our ancestors had a fatalistic outlook on life, as if you could imagine any of them just lying down to die. In fact, Viking believed that one's fate was hardly more important than what one did with one's fate; the attitude of how you faced that fate. There is no honor in passively surrendering to fate. Honor is found in approaching one's fate as a battle to be fought, even if that battle is doomed to failure. Just as the gods approach their own doom at Ragnarok. What we have is a very complex and entwined philosophy that is found within the concepts of Wyrd and Orlog.

To understand Wyrd, you must first understand Orlog. In various sources, we are told that the Norns choose life, meaning that they determine when and where a person will be born. By making this determination the Norns choose the individual person's Orlog. This Orlog should be viewed as the mold that will shape that particular life. Orlog is laid upon us due to the circumstances of our birth, and the Wyrd that the Norns have laid out for us to follow. The Norns pick the time, the place, and to a certain extent the family you will be born into. They even choose the time of your death, but they do not choose how our lives will end.

They regulate and shape your Wyrd up to the point when you begin to react to your environment and the conditions set in front of you. But there are many decisions to be made between the crib and the grave. As your current actions become your past, they shape each and every moment of your current existence. How you react or what you do at any given moment will become a future with consequences. Every decision you make shapes your future and impacts that final aspect of your Wyrd and the Orlog that you leave for your future generations.

You may have heard the phrase, "Who you are today is based on the actions you took five years ago." Today it is a common theme with motivational circles, but the idea is rooted in ancient heathen belief systems. What you do today will indeed shape the person and the circumstances of your life in five years.

Wyrd is the past actions that create and shape the present as well as the future. Our ancestors viewed our actions like rocks being dropped into a pond, our deeds ripple outward. We affect those closest to us first and more strongly, but then our impact and influence reach out to the edges of the pond.

Consider time not as a swiftly flowing river constantly rushing us further away from our birth and to our death, but instead it is a lake or pool of infinite size. A handful of pebbles tossed onto the surface creates simultaneous, rippling impressions on the water that spread out, touch, and overlap. Each pebble is a distinct individual's separate action. They may be larger or smaller, and they may create splashes that are greater or lesser in size, but each one creates an impression on every other pebble that hits the water. These pebbles represent Wyrd and how and where these pebbles hit the surface of the water are dictated by our actions.

Choose your actions wisely and fight against the death that is foretold for everything in the universe. We cannot change when the ending comes but we can face it bravely and with honor. Until that end comes, live your life to the best of your ability. Your actions have an important impact on your future and the ripples you make in the well of Wyrd touch more than you know.

The Self/Soul

Let's first do away with the word "soul" because it is a foreign concept within the Heathen belief system. The various heathenistic views have never placed much value on a uniform set of doctrines and therefore there is not a dogmatic account of the different parts of the human self. This is not to say that we are not completely lacking in references; the resources are simply limited in scope and uniformity. What we do know is that the Self is made up of different aspects that co-exist with one another, and yet can also exist separately on their own. This is why when you first discover the concept of the heathen Self it is difficult to understand. We have been so indoctrinated into as a oneness that it is now hard for us to grasp and understand what our ancestors once thought and believed.

At our core of beliefs is the concept of Wyrd or Orlog. This is the force in the universe that determines the Self and our perceptions of it.

By describing the most important and commonly mentioned parts of the Self, we hope you will discover a deeper understanding of what it means to be Heathen.

- **Lich – Physical Body**
- **Hamr – Shape, Form, Appearance**
- **Hugr – Thought**
- **Frlgja – Follower**
- **Hamingja – Luck**

Lich is the physical shape in which we walk around in the physical world. This physical body is the vessel that contains all the various aspects that truly make up what is the Self.

Hamr is one's form or appearance, that which can be perceived through sensory observation. Unlike the modern view; that which is perceived by the senses is not always fixed into a single unchangeable form. The Norse believe that someone can change their Hamr and how it is perceived by another person's senses. The ability to do this is called hamramr; which means that someone has a very strong Hamr. The Hamr is different than the Lich. The Lich is the physical body whereas the Hamr is the perception of an appearance.

Hugr can be most satisfactorily translated into thought or mind. It corresponds to someone's personality and their conscious thought. It therefore overlaps considerable with what we would think of as someone's inner self. The Hugr generally stays within its owner, but at times it can create certain effects on distant people just by thinking of them in a specific way. This is particularly possible if a person has an exceptionally strong Hugr.

Fylgja is generally perceived in an animal form by those who can see with what is commonly called second sight. It is not completely unheard of for a Fylgja to be in a human form but it is rare. It is thought to be an attendant personification whose well-being is intimately tied to that of the person it is attached to; for example, if the Fylgja dies then the host will die as well. Its character and form are closely connected to the character and traits that are embodied by its host. Fylgja translates as a follower but that seems a little misleading because it is often depicted as traveling ahead to arrive at a destination before the person it is attached to. It can also be seen appearing in the dreams of someone who is destined to meet the connected host in the near future.

Hamingja is often used in an abstract way to signify luck but the heathen concept of luck is very different from other cultures. Luck is the quality that is inherent in a man and woman along with their family lineage. It is a part of one's personality that corresponds to one's strength, intelligence, and skill. It is at once both the cause and the expression of the success, wealth and power of the family. Your inherent success in life is shaped by your Hamingja while at the same time; it is being formed by your life. Hamingja is a personal entity in its own right. It is a part of the Self that can split off from the other components in certain situations. As such, it will grow and develop before finally passing its attributes down through your family line upon your death.

THE NINE WORLDS

- ASGARD — HOME OF THE AESIR
- MUSPELLHEIM — HOME OF THE FIRE GIANTS AND DEMONS
- ALFHEIM — HOME OF THE LIGHT ELVES
- MIDGARD — HOME OF HUMANS
- VANAHEIM — HOME OF THE VANIR
- NIDAVELLIR — HOME OF THE DWARVES
- HELHEIM — HOME OF HEL AND THE DISHONORABLE DEAD
- JOTUNHEIM — HOME OF THE GIANTS
- NIFLHEIM — WORLD OF ICE, FOG, AND MIST

The Nine Worlds Within Us

Niflheim -- The unconscious (misty) spiritual realm of the unkind (frozen) soul. The home of mist and darkness.

Jotunheim -- The non-conscious outer world of the frost/rock, earth/hateful spirits of the naked ego and the extinguished soul. World of the frost giants.

Helheim -- The semi-conscious/sub-conscious spiritual realms of the dead, (foggy mental landscape/barren. wasteland of ever diminishing folk memory). World of the dead.

Asgard -- The folk conscious overworld of perfect righteousness enlightenment, alignment with nature, truth, justice, and blood virtue. World of the Aesir.

Muspellheim -- The unconscious (dark) spiritual realm of the psychotic/ destructive (fiery) spirits of the naked eye. Home of element fire, and the fire giants

Vanaheim -- The folk detached/transcendent overworld of misplaced righteousness (domain of Vanir). World of Vanir

Midgard -- The visible middle world of reality, the ancestral domain of an embattled mankind (eternal struggle for life/power). Middle garden, land of men.

Ljossalfheim --The short sighted/diminutive outer world of self-righteousness/false pride/ideals rooted in exaggerated self-importance. Home to the Fairies and the Elves.

Svartalfheim -- The dark home/diminutive subterranean underworld of the dwarf, dark elves/spirits of envy, selfish desire, corruption, racial decomposition. World of the Dwarfs, Trolls and Gnomes

Runes

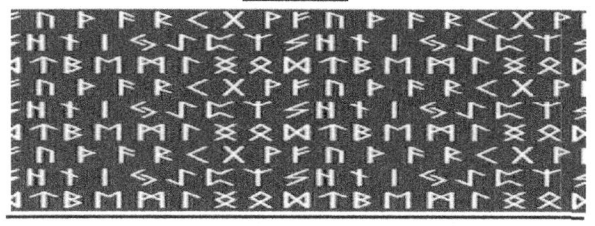

The runic system is known as the futhark from the first six symbols of the first aett; just as our current system of writing is called the alphabet after the first two letters of the Roman lettering system: alpha and beta.

Where, when and how the runic system originated is still a subject of debate. Roughly a third of the futhark may have derived from Latin, but other languages, Greek, Etruscan and north Italian have been brought into the mix, as well as the writing styles of the Celts, Goths, Marcomanni and Eruli. Where so much is uncertain it is easier to just say the futhark is based upon one or more Southern European systems of writing.

The shapes of the runes are based on vertical and diagonal strokes to make it easier to carve on wood and stone. The easiest datable runic inscriptions are found in Denmark but this does not rule out a contemporary usage among the Goths north of the Black Sea. Some scholars stress the magical significance of the runes, and there is no doubt that the runes were used for spells, magical castings, and divination. But runes were an all-purpose writing system and were frequently used for gnomic, commemorative, recording and identifying purposes. The range and number of runic inscriptions is impressive: from Greenland to the Black Sea, from Isle of Man to Athens; they are found in Iceland, Denmark, Norway, Sweden and with a little controversy, even North America.

Runes are some of the most powerful symbols of what it means to be Heathen. The word "rune" literally means mystery and represents that murky darkness of the mystical unknown. This murky path leads back to the beginning of the runes and the first developments of a spirituality that you are currently exploring.

It begins with Odin and his insatiable thirst for knowledge. Allfather has always been relentless in his pursuit of answers, to all questions. He has never balked at the necessary sacrifices he has had to make, nor hesitated at the distance he has had to travel. This endless quest brought about his greatest achievement since he and his brothers overthrew the giant Ymir and created Midgard from his corpse.

His obsession for knowledge drove him to the very center of reality, to the great tree Yggdrasil. Where its limbs stretched out to the very corners of the universe, and touched upon all the known realms of existence. Inspired by its hallowed limbs and vast expanse, he made a sacrifice of himself to himself.

He took up his spear, pierced his own flesh and let the blood flow before hanging himself alongside the mighty trunk. There he remained, between the worlds, between realities, between life and death, for nine days and nights, without food and water. On the final day he looked up into the branches of the cosmic tree, and the mystical shapes, pulsing with power, were revealed to him. Even now, every tree in Midgard carries these ancient symbols within their branches. Go, stand beneath the branches and look up. The runes are there, shaped by the branches and the leaves, waiting for you to discover them.

When Odin saw them and recognized their power, he screamed out rapturously, and took up this new knowledge. He climbed down from his place of self-sacrifice and snapped off a branch from the steed of revelation. He carved twenty-four runes onto the branch, creating a magical rod known as a Gandrstaff. He split the runes into three equal columns and called each set an Aett, which means family. So every group of eight runes is listed within a family. Related, connected, telling their own story to you as you gain a deeper understanding of them, and the universe that you inhabit.

Continue to study, to know, every step will reveal more to you. For now, I give you a brief introduction to the runes, and a very basic way to appreciate and learn to interpret them.

The first one is the simplest and most basic; it's what I call the Mimir pull. Named after Mimir's well of knowledge and the sacrifice Odin had to make to get a single drink. In this version though, no one has to lose an eye, but you can only take a single rune, as Odin could only take that single drink.

It's simple. Open up your rune bag, breathe in, and exhale into your bag three times while concentrating on the question you want an answer to. Pull the bag away and reach inside. One rune will attract your fingers. Pull it out, and then look for the interpretation of that particular rune. This pull is meant to give you a quick, brief answer. It may only be a glimpse, but sometimes a peek is all you need.

If you need a little more though, well then we have another easy to do pull. I call this one the Norn pull, because for this one, you pull out three runes. One for the past, one for the present and one for the future. You can begin this one either of two ways, both are acceptable. The first way is just like you did with the Mimir pull. You exhale into your rune bag three times while concentrating on your question. If your rune bag is big enough and you prefer, you can reach in and stir the runes around while focusing on the question you want answers to. Stir until you feel the urge to stop, and then pull out three runes one at a time, and lay them down from left to right. The furthest left represents the past, the middle one is the present, and the furthest to the right is the future.

The past should give you some kind of indication of how you arrived at your current situation. The middle one is giving you advice, and the one to the right is telling you how the situation will turn out. If you are confused by any of the runes in front of you, or you need further clarification, draw one more. Place this rune above the one that is causing you confusion, hopefully it helps.

Regardless of the method that you choose to use, the runes provide information and clarification because they can provoke or prod you into considering other possibilities. They often inspire me to seek out solutions that I may never have considered. If nothing else they can open your mind to different paths you can take when facing challenges.

Your ancestors studied and read these runes in a similar fashion. Feel that call and always follow your intuition when approaching the runes. They are defined as a mystery for a reason and the results may surprise you.

Do you hear the wind as it blows through the branches of the trees? Do you see it as it moves the leaves? Do you feel it on the skin of your cheek?

It is the voice of Odin and he speaks to the blood of your ancestor, the same blood that flows through your veins. It is the voice that makes you question. It is the sound that makes your heart beat faster. It is the feeling that sets your soul on fire and lifts it up.

Frey's Aett
Feju (F)

Traditional Meaning – Cattle/Moveable Wealth
God/Goddess- Njord, Frey, Freyja
Element – Fire
Color – Fiery Red
Stone – Carnelian

The first rune in the elder futhark means cattle, but in the context of it being something of value that can be moved from one location to the next. In our modern idea of that concept we could make the mistake of limiting our thoughts to a strictly financial view, i.e. money. Take a deeper look though; focus on the connection to Njord, Frey and Freyja. There is a fertility concept lying just below the surface. You plant a crop so that you can reap later on. You breed cattle to increase your heard. Don't overlook this view when approaching this rune. Yes, it may be financial, but it may include the concept of prudent planting, or careful breeding that will increase your wealth.

Uruz (U)

Traditional Meaning – Aurochs/Primal Strength
God/Goddess – Thor
Element – Earth
Color – Red
Stone – Tiger's Eye

    This second rune is named after the primal wild ox that was native to Northern Europe, the Auroch. The Auroch was six feet tall at the shoulders and covered in long, shaggy black hair with massive, curved horns. It is now extinct, but it once held a very sacred position in European cultures. Think of the first creature in the universe, Audhumla, and the strength that Thor brings to the table. This rune embodies that natural strength, that raw natural power that exists within nature and lends itself to all. This rune may be telling you to be strong, or it may be telling you to embrace your own inner strength.

Thurisaz (TH)

Traditional Meaning: Giant/Protection
God/Goddess – Thor
Element – Fir
Color – Red
Stone – Bloodstone

This rune traditionally means giant and therefore represents a destructive or chaotic element. On the other hand, we know that Thor is protector against those forces. This rune is like a thorn on a rose, which it resembles, or like Thor's hammer. They both harm and protect simultaneously without conflicting with their nature. This rune protects as it harms, but the harm done is in aid of its duty to protect. Look closely, the harm you have recently went through may have long term benefits for you.

Ansuz (A)

Traditional Meaning – Voice of God
God/Goddess – Odin
Element – Air
Color – Indigo
Stone – Lapis

This rune represents communication but because of its connection to Odin, it is inspirational in nature. Think of that inner voice that urges and motivates you to strive for more. This rune embodies Odin's knowledge and wisdom because it is this voice that drove him to seek it. This is the spark that pushes you to achieve, the one that lifts you up and moves you to write that piece of poetry. This is the rune that motivates. Listen to it, feel it.

Raido (R)

Traditional Meaning – Movement/Journey
God/Goddess – Thor
Element – Fire/Air
Color – Red
Stone – Turquoise

This rune is all about movement, a forward journey. Raido is never stagnant, it is constantly moving through both time and space. It is a rune of action, just like the god it is associated with. This rune is telling you to take charge of your own path. It is telling you that you are in charge of what direction your life takes. Maybe you have stumbled off the path you began travelling down or maybe it is time to take a different road. No matter the course you take, this rune is reminding you that you are in charge of your journey. It could also be telling you that you are about to travel.

Kenaz (K)

Traditional Meaning – Torch/Light
God/Goddess – Heimdall, Freyja
Element – Fire
Color – Red/Orange
Stone – Flint/Opal

The traditional meaning of this rune is torch or light, but it means to know or be familiar with. The way you would know a room or become familiar with the contents of that room if you flipped the light on. Take it one step further and apply it to the light of inspiration, or the spark of creativity. Knowledge can also be the torch that lights up the world and helps you to both know and become more familiar with it. Kenaz is the torch that illuminates your life and makes it more knowable. This rune is leading you to the understanding that will give your life that deeper meaning. This rune is telling you to seek more knowledge, develop a deeper understanding of the situation.

Gebo (G)

Traditional Meaning – Gift
God/Goddess – Odin
Element – Air
Color – Blue/Gold
Stone – Emerald

Gebo means gift, but also means exchange. According to our beliefs and culture, the act of giving is never one sided. A gift is given with the understanding that a gift will be given in return. The same when you make a sacrifice to the gods. You do this with a clear expectation of something in return. Usually that means a good crop, prosperity, or even a happy marriage. Therefore, this is the rune of sacrifice, exchange, and loyalty. Loyalty because that is also something that is given with an expected return. A gift for a gift is a profound concept that reaches far deeper than the currently viewed sacrifice. To receive a gift, to give a gift, the exchange if done properly will always bring a smile to all participants. Are you about to receive a gift, or is it time to return one?

Wunjo (W or V)

Traditional Meaning – Joy
God/Goddess – Odin
Element- Air
Color – Gold
Stone- Topaz/Rose Quartz

This is the last rune of the first aett, and it means joy, but it also has been translated to mean glory and perfection.

Wunjo is about personal wholeness and the will to strive for perfection. Not perfection or wholeness as seen through another's eyes, but through your own. It is about joy, your own personal joy. You can only find true happiness within yourself. This is the rune of harmony and unity, which brings about true joy. This rune is either telling you that you are happy, happiness is coming or that you need to seek balance.

Hagal's Aett

Hagalaz (H)
Traditional Meaning – Hail
God/Goddess- Hel, Frigga
Element – Water
Color – Grey
Stone – Crystal

The traditional meaning of this rune is hail, or hailstone. Hail is definitely a sign of chaos and destruction. Most often it is seen as the wrath of frozen water falling from the sky, beating down fields of grain with forceful violence. This destruction though gives the soil more nutrients and brings about the potential for more abundant growth later on. This rune could represent growth through struggle or destruction. Its association with the goddess Hel and Frigga gives us a clue. Hel is the goddess of the dead and Frigga is the goddess of birth. There could be a rebirth in the making, something reawakening.

Nauthiz (N)
Traditional meaning – Need
God/Goddess- Skuld
Element – Fire
Color – Black
Stone – Obsidian

This rune resembles the bow drill that is used to start fires. Fire is essential for survival, but this rune also has a strong connection to the Norn, Skuld. This particular Norn is an aspect of fate. She represents the future, and need is also a concept that is constantly pulling us forward. This rune may be telling you that something is necessary, or something about your future. Look to your needs and pay attention to the future.

Isa (I)
Traditional Meaning – Ice
God/Goddess – Verdani, Skadi
Element – Water
Color- White
Stone – Herkimer Diamond

Ice is of course frozen water, and can be viewed as a negative, as if you are stuck, frozen and immobile, or like ice it could be preservation. Isa has a strong connection to the winter loving Skadi, she is a huntress who must move cautiously. Combine that with this rune's connection to the Norn Verdandi, who represents the present, and you have a rune that could be telling you to pay attention to your current situation and move carefully.

Jera (J or Y)

Traditional Meaning – Year/Harvest
God/Goddess – Frey, Freyja
Element – Earth
Color- Green
Stone – Agate

Jera represents the cycle of the year, therefore the seasons, coming to a complete circle. This is the rune to draw above your front door to ensure a good year. Take ashes, mix with water and on the first day of the New Year, draw it above the door. This rune speaks of a good year and a rich harvest, but always remember that a rich harvest has to be cultivated and worked at. Never take anything for granted, put in the effort and the rewards will follow. This rune may be telling you that a cycle is starting or coming to an end.

Eihwaz (Ei)

Traditional Meaning – Yew
God/Goddess – Odin, Uller, Skadi
Element – Air
Color – Green
Stone – Smoky Quartz

This rune represents the Yew tree. The Yew is an evergreen tree with bright red berries and a very strong elastic wood. Its wood was used to make bows that were greatly prized for their strength. Eihwaz is a rune of endurance and a strongly rooted center, suggesting a point of strength and the qualities needed to persevere. This rune's strong connection to Uller and Skadi speaks of strength and endurance. This god and goddess live high in the isolated wilderness, through snowy passes they hunt and survive. This rune could be telling you that through your strength you will endure whatever is currently happening.

Pertho (P)
Traditional Meaning – Lot Cup
God/Goddess – Mimir, Frigga, The Norns
Element – Water
Color- Silver
Stone – Onyx

Pertho has always had an obscure meaning, but most associate it with a lot cup, the dice that goes into it, and a game of chance. Most people view the concept of fate as someing you cannot change it. Look to whom it is associated with though, Frigga is the goddess who brings something into the world whether that is the birth of a child or an idea. Mimir is the guardian of the well of wisdom, and the Norns represent the past, present, and future. Grab your fate by your own hands, take a chance but be wise in doing so.

Elhaz (Z)

Traditional Meaning – Elk
God/Goddess – Heimdall, The Valkyries
Element – Air/Fire
Color- Rainbow
Stone – Black Tourmaline

    This rune is symbolic of a splayed hand or an elk's antlers, both are signs of protection. It is more than protection though; it is an inner peace, a calm connection with nature. The elk traveling though the woods on a foggy morning or that open hand spread out in a friendly wave. This rune was once used to mark graves, hence its association with the Valkyries, and the rainbow bridge. This rune brings on the feeling of peace and tranquility by offering overwhelming protection. This rune can ward and create a holy sanctuary, so be calm, everything is going to be okay. Relax.

Sowilo (S)

Traditional Meaning – Sun
God/Goddess – Heimdall, Thor, Balder
Element – Fire
Color – Gold
Stone – Norse Sunstone

    Sowilo is the rune of the life-giving sun and is represented as a ray of that very sun. It is the bringer of organic life as it melts the ice of winter to bring about a fresh spring. This rune can also be related to the sun's progress as it cycles through the year. This is both a guide and a path that can lead those who are seeking inspiration and a brighter future. This is a rune of success and victory. A hopeful rune that brings good tidings.

Tyr's Aett

Tiwaz (T)

Traditional Meaning – Tyr
God/Goddess – Tyr
Element – Air
Color – Red
Stone- Bloodstone/Star Ruby

Tyr is the god of justice, courage, and self-sacrifice, but he is also the god of victory. This rune was often considered the rune of victory and our ancestors would carve it onto their weapons as an appeal to him. This rune is said to immolate Tyr's attributes as well as his sense of justice, but do not take this to mean the coded rules of law. Tyr is the god of natural justice which means right and wrong and survival of the fittest. This rune may be telling you to have courage in the face of sacrifice. Or like our ancestors believed, it may be telling you that victory is at hand if you remain courageous.

Berkana (B)
Traditional Meaning – Birch
God/Goddess – Nerthus, Freyja, Frigga
Element – Earth
Color – Green
Stone – Jet

This is the rune of the birch tree. It is a symbol of renewal and growth. It carries with it the potential for new life, possibilities, and new beginnings. Berkana is definitely a rune that belongs to the goddesses in all of their fertility related aspects. This rune may simply represent an awakening, a deeper understanding as it is also seen as a symbol of Spring. Look to its connections to the goddesses, it may be a symbol of fertility or the growth of a planted seed. It could be a symbol of change, new possibilities, or an upcoming birth.

Ehwaz (E)
Traditional Meaning – Horse/ Cooperation
God/Goddess – Frey, Freyja, Odin
Element – Earth
Color – Green
Stone – Turquoise

Ehwaz is the rune of the horse. Horses were not only means of travel, but also a source of prosperity and joy. They were also held to be a very scared animal. The horse was viewed as a blend of power and divine inspiration, because just like a ship it has the ability to bear the soul from one world to another. For this animal to be truly useful though there must be cooperation between it and its rider. With this powerful symbolism and its connection to Frey and Freyja this rune as well as the horse embrace fertility. Odin is inspiration, combined with the horse and fertility and you have potential. This is the beginning of a new chapter, but it must be done in cooperation with the previous one.

Mannaz (M)

Traditional Meaning – Mankind
God/Goddess – Heimdall, Mimir
Element – Air
Color – Blue
Stone – Amethyst

    Mannaz represents humanity in a large general way, but also represents the interaction of mankind. The greatest joy of man, according to the Havamal is sharing space and time with other people. A flame is kindled by a flame, and a man becomes clever by talking with another man. Man is the joy of man. Loneliness can dull the mind as well as your outlook on life. Take a look at your surroundings and your close associations, something may need to be changed.

Laguz (L)

Traditional Meaning – Lake/ Water
God/Goddess – Njord, Ran
Element – Water
Color – Sea
Stone – Malachite

    Laguz is the rune of water, but more specifically it represents the great unknown that lies in the deep depths. It is the awe-inspiring vastness and power of the ocean. Its association with Njord and Ran can also represent turbulence, like a wind tossed sea, or the doomed sailors drawn into her depths with her mighty net so that they can live in her coral halls. This does not mean that Laguz is a rune of death, or life, because water is also life. It means a change and probably a change that will come with rough waters.

Ingwaz (NG)

Traditional Meaning – Frey
God/Goddess – Frey
Element – Earth
Color – Green
Stone – Ivory

    One of Frey's ancient names is Ingvi Frey, so this rune is strongly associated with the fertility god. The general meaning of this rune is potentially energy, which makes sense with its association with the god of fertility. It is like a seed that must undergo a gestation period to come into its full being. This is like the work that you must put into a project before it reaches its full potential. This is the rune that lets you know that your seed is gestating, waiting as stored energy until it has been released.

Dagaz (D)

Traditional Meaning – Day
God/Goddess – Heimdall, Loki
Element – Fire/Air
Color – Red
Stone – Fluorite

This rune carries with it the promise of the coming light. A new day filled with new beginnings and the potential to be anything. This could be that revelation that Loki is often responsible for, or an epiphany in regard to an old idea. This rune represents that fresh feeling when you face that indrawn breath of a new dawn, or that glimpse of a rainbow after a cleansing rain. This is a bright day filled with hope.

Othala (O)
Traditional Meaning - Heritage/Property
God/Goddess – Odin
Element – Earth
Color – Red
Stone – Petrified Wood

    This is the final rune in the Elder Futhark and as such it represents the end with the thought of the heritage it is passing along. Heritage and inherited land used to be synonymous with each other because families never left the lands they were born onto. Generations remained in the same areas, always improving for the future while keeping an eye on the past. Othala is representative of that very idea. It is the heritage and property that is left to you, and what you will leave behind to the next generation. Othala should be viewed with that stability in mind, as well as its impact. The future is created from the past.

Overview Gods and Goddesses

Name	Meaning
❋ Aegir	God of the deep seas
❋ Balder	God of light and beauty
❋ Bertha	Goddess and protector of unborn children
❋ Bragi	God of eloquence and poetry
❋ Eir	Goddess of healing
❋ Forseti	God of judicial law and order
❋ Frey	God of fertility and lust
❋ Frigga	Goddess of matrimonial love and the home
❋ Freyja	Goddess of sexual desire & magic
❋ Gefion	Goddess of pregnancy
❋ Heimdall	God of protection and guardian of the Bifrost bridge
❋ Hel	Goddess of the dead
❋ Hermod	Odin's son and messenger of the Gods

- Hodur — God of darkness and blind chance that occurs in battle
- Hoenir — One of the creators of man, giver of Motion
- Idunna — Goddess of fruitfulness and youth
- Lofn — Goddess of secret and illicit love affairs
- Loki — God of mischief and the hearth fire
- Nanna — Goddess of joy and devotion
- Njord — God of wind, waves, and the sea close to shore
- Nott — Goddess of night
- Odin — God of wisdom, runes, & war
- Ostara — Goddess of Spring
- Ran — Goddess of the sea depths and collector of drowned sailors
- Saga — Goddess of history
- Sif — Goddess of the harvest
- Sigyn — Represents the loyal and devoted wife
- Skadi — Goddess of winter and the hunt
- Snotra — Goddess of virtue and master of all knowledge
- Syn — Goddess of truth and the guardian of the door to Frigga's place
- Thor — God of storms, thunder, and lighting
- Tyr — God of war, sacrifice, and victory

- Uller — God of duels, winter, and hunting
- Vali — God of vengeance
- Var — Goddess of oaths and punisher of perjurers
- Vor — Goddess of faith
- Vidar — God of silence and revenge
- Vjofn — Goddess of peace and Concord

The Goddesses

The goddesses of Heathen are not passive entities. They are powerful beings with their own roles, properties and palaces. They are the representatives of the values that we hold and their words carry just as much weight as their male counterparts. They are even designated with their own name they are collectively known as the Asynjur. They are also the most likely to collect the souls of the dead and give them safe places to enjoy eternal peace.

It is unfortunate but most of their stories were erased by an invading force that feared powerful women. It is disappointing because the goddesses are just as important to our history and to our future as the gods are. In this list, I hope you find the inspiration you need to feel their presence and to seek them out on your own spiritual quest.

Frigga

- Goddess of the sky, marriage and motherhood
- Queen of Asgard
- Tall, beautiful with white hair and bright blue eyes.
- Often portrayed wearing a silver dress or a long evergreen colored dress with a tan apron.
- Her crown is made from Heron plumes because they are a symbol of silence.

- She carries a ring of keys that are symbolic of her role as head of the household.
- She possesses the knowledge of the future, but never reveals what she knows.
- Watches over the souls of unborn children.
- Fensalir is where husbands and wives go when they do not wish to be parted in death.
- Fensalir   Palace
- Fiorgyn   Father
- Odin   Husband
- Balder   Son with Odin
- Hermod   Son with Odin
- Hodur   Son with Odin

Fulla

- Described as very beautiful with long golden hair that hangs loose only restrained by a golden circlet.
- Her hair is emblematic of golden grain
- She is considered the symbol of the fullness of Earth
- Confidante and trusted advisor to Frigga
- Frigga   Sister

Gna

- Frigga's messenger
- She can travel through fire and air, over land and sea and is considered the representation of the refreshing breeze.

- 🍂 She sees all that happens on Earth and reports it all to Frigga.
- 🍂 Hofvarpnir		Horse

Vjofn

- 🍂 Goddess of peace and love
- 🍂 She opens stubborn hearts to love.
- 🍂 She is in charge of maintaining peace and concord among mankind.
- 🍂 She reconciles quarreling husband and wives.

Var

- 🍂 Goddess of honesty and troth
- 🍂 She hears all oaths and punishes perjurers, while rewarding those who keep their word.

Snotra

- 🍂 Goddess of Virtue
- 🍂 She is said to have mastered all knowledge
- 🍂 Her name roughly translates to Prudent

Vor

- 🍂 Goddess of intuition

- It is said that she knows all that is to occur throughout the world.

Ostara

- Goddess of Spring, rebirth and fertility
- She is often accompanied by rabbits and storks, the symbols for new life.

Hlin

- Goddess of consolation
- She kisses away the tears of mourners and pours balm into the hearts of those who have been wrung by grief.
- She also carries prayers to Frigga and advises her on how to give the desired relief.

Gefjon

- Her name translates to the giving one.
- To her are entrusted all the maidens that die unwedded.
- She hosts them in the halls of Fensalir.

Eira

- Goddess of Healing
- She gathers samples from all over to heal wounds and cure diseases

- She teaches her science to those who practice medicine.

Saga

- Goddess of history
- Odin goes to drink with her on a regular basis so that she can tell him the stories of the past as they occur.
- Sokkvabekk   Palace

Idunna

- Goddess of youth and spring
- Keeper of the golden apples
- Long blonde wavy hair with honey colored eyes.
- Voluptuous and youthful
- Most often seen in loose fitting white sundress with white flowers in her hair.
- Bragi   Husband
- Lives in the groves of Brunnaker

Sigyn

- Her names translates to Friend of Victory
- She is the representation of a loving and devoted wife
- Loki   Husband
- Narvi   Son with Loki
- Vali   Son with Loki

Sif

- She is the embodiment of the fertile Earth
- Her long golden hair is the symbol of ripe golden wheat
- Thor — Husband
- Uller — Son, born before married to Thor
- Lorride — Daughter with Thor
- Thrud — Daughter with Thor

Nanna

- Goddess of purity, joy and devotional love
- Known for her beauty and charm
- Her name means Blossom
- Nip — Father
- Balder — Husband
- Forseti — Son with Balder

Freyja

- Goddess of beauty, sexual desire and magic
- Queen of the Valkyries
- Often portrayed wearing a corset and helmet while carrying a shield and spear
- Long black hair, milky white skin and bright green eyes.
- She has a feathered cloak that transforms whoever wears it into a falcon.

- Two large grey cats pull her chariot
- She collects the first half of the warriors who die in battle
- Njord — Father
- Nerthus — Mother
- Frey — Brother
- Odur — Husband
- Hnoss — Daughter with Odur
- Gersemi — Daughter with Odur
- Brisingamen — Necklace
- Hildisvini — Boar
- Folkvang — Realm
- Sessrymnir — Palace

Skadi

- Goddess of winter and the hunt
- Inventor of snowshoes
- She has long white hair in a braid and has silver eyes
- Her clothing is white leather, augmented with white and grey furs
- She carries both a bow and a sword
- Accompanied by three grey wolves with silver collars
- Thiassi — Father
- Njord — Ex-husband
- Uller — Husband
- Thrymheim — Castle

Nerthus

- She is a Vanir goddess so she is heavily connected to fertility and the earth itself.
- She is described as being very tan with dark brown hair and black eyes
- Njord   Brother/Ex-husband
- Frey   Son with Njord
- Freyja   Daughter with Njord

Ran

- Goddess of the sea and the drowned
- Her name translates as Robber
- Her palace is in the coral caves where those who perish at sea go.
- She has nine daughters with Aegir. They collectively gave birth to Heimdall:

    | Gialp | Greip | Egia |
    | Augeia | Ulfrun | Aurgiafa |
    | Sindur | Atla | Iarnsaxa |

- Aegir   Husband/Brother
- Loki   Brother

Hel

- Goddess of the afterlife and reincarnation

- Queen of the dead
- She is described as being beautiful but half living and half dead with cat-like green eyes and raven black hair
- Angurboda   Mother
- Loki   Father
- Fenris   Brother
- Iormungandr   Brother
- Elvidner   Great hall
- Garm   Guardian Hound

Lofn

- Her name means love.
- Her duty is to remove obstacles from the path of lovers.
- She helps forbidden lovers to the marriage alter.

Syn

- Goddess of defense
- Her names means Truth
- She guards the door to Frigga's palace and refuses to open it for anyone not allowed in.
- Presides over tribunals and trials.

The Gods

The gods are divided into two separate groups or tribes, the Aesir and the Vanir. The Aesir is said to represent martial strength and to embody the ruling class, while the Vanir embody nature and fertility. The truth is that neither of these tribes can be restricted in such a way. They are individuals and as such, there is a lot of crossover and most often, each god plays a duel role that cannot easily be isolated to one ideal tribe. Both groups preserve the past, even sharing in roles for collecting and caring for the souls of the dead, while at the same time guaranteeing that there will be crops for the future. The aspects and personalities of the gods are not meant to be static. They are always changing, evolving, adapting to the worlds around them. Study and learning from each, as you too change, evolve and adapt.

Odin

- God of wisdom, runes, the hanged, battle, sacrifice & death.
- Heroic warriors who fall in battle go to his hall, Valhalla.
- Portrayed as having long black and grey hair and beard, or with a shaved head and long beard. He only has one blue eye. He looks like a powerfully built man in his fifties.

- Bor — Father
- Bestla — Mother
- Vili — Brother
- Ve — Brother
- Frigga — Wife
- Balder — Son with Frigga
- Hoder — Son with Frigga
- Hermod — Son with Frigga
- Vali — Son with Rinda
- Vidar — Son with Grid
- Heimdall — Son with Nine Wave Maidens
- Bragi — Son with Gunnlod
- Thor — Son with Jord
- Loki — Bloodbrother
- Sleipnir — Horse
- Gungnir — Spear
- Draupnir — Arm ring
- Hlidskialf — Throne
- Valhalla — Great Hall
- Geri — Wolf
- Freki — Wolf

- Hugin — Raven
- Munin — Raven

Thor

- God of Thunder, lightning, storms, and soldiers
- Bilskirnir is also a place for the dead; soldiers, farmers, servants, and those dedicated to Thor.
- Described as a large warrior with long red hair and beard with fierce blue eyes.
- Odin — Father
- Jord — Mother
- Sif — Wife
- Uller — Step-son
- Thrud — Daughter with Sif
- Lorride — Daughter with Sif
- Magni — Son with Iarnsaxa
- Modi — Son with Iarnsaxa
- Thialfi — Servant/ward
- Roskva — Servant/ward
- Tanngiostr — Goat/Ram
- Tanngrisnir — Goat/Ram
- Thrudheim — Realm
- Bilskirnir — Hall
- Mjollnir — Hammer
- Iarngreiper — Magical gloves
- Megingiord — Magical belt

Hodur

- God of Darkness and blind chance
- Described as somber, taciturn and blind
- Odin	Father
- Frigga	Mother
- Balder	Brother
- Hermod	Brother

Frey

- God of fruitfulness, peace and prosperity
- Green eyes, long rich brown hair and trimmed beard
- Njord	Father
- Nerthus	Mother
- Freyja	Sister
- Gerda	Wife
- Fiolnir	Son of Gerda
- Skirnir	Servant
- Beyggvir	Attendant
- Beyla	Attendant
- Ljosalfheim	Realm
- Skidbladnir	Magical ship
- Gullinbursti	Boar
- Blodughofi	Horse

Bragi

- God of poetry, music and eloquence
- Famous for his wisdom
- His name means the foremost one
- Represented with long white hair and matching long white beard
- Never far from his harp
- Odin   Father
- Gunnlod   Mother
- Idunna   Wife

Balder

- God of light, innocence and the new spring
- Described as the most beautiful of gods, he has white-blonde hair and shining blue eyes
- Odin   Father
- Frigga   Mother
- Hodur   Brother
- Hermod   Brother
- Nanna   Wife
- Forseti   Son with Nanna
- Hringhorni   Ship
- Breidablik   Palace

Forseti

- God of justice, righteousness, and judicial proceedings
- The legal disputes that he oversees are always reconciled to the satisfaction of everyone involved.
- Wields a golden battle-axe
- Balder	Father
- Nanna	Mother
- Glitnir	Palace

Vali

- God of eternal light
- The avenger of Balder
- Represented and worshipped as an archer
- His arrows represent beams of light
- The harbinger of brighter days
- Odin	Father
- Rinda	Mother
- Valaskialf	Dwelling

Uller

- God of hunting, archery, winter and single combat
- Also known as the shield-god when being invoked by people about to engage in single combat.
- Dresses in heavy furs, carries a bow and arrows and noted for his use of skis and ice skates.

- Sif — Mother
- Thor — Step-Father
- Skadi — Wife
- Ydalir — The vale of Yews where he makes his home.

Njord

- God of the sea winds, coastal oceans, commerce, prosperity and fishing
- Handsome with brown hair, eyes the color of seaweed and most often depicted wearing the same seaweed colored clothing
- Nerthus — First wife/sister
- Frey — Son with Nerthus
- Freyja — Daughter with Nerthus
- Skadi — Second wife/divorced
- Noatun — Palace

Loki

- God of mischief, hearth fire and the spirit of life
- Portrayed as smooth faced. Fiery-orange hair, pointy nose. Tall and skinny with very dark eyes
- Shape shifter
- Farbauti — Father
- Laufey — Mother
- Aegir — Brother

- Ran — Sister
- Odin — Bloodbrother
- Glut — First wife
- Eisa — Daughter with Glut
- Einmyria — Daughter with Glut
- Angurboda — Second wife
- Hel — Daughter with Angurboda
- Iormungandr — Son with Angurboda
- Fenris — Son with Angurboda
- Sigyn — Third wife
- Narve — Son with Sigyn
- Vali — Son with Sigyn
- Sleipnir — Son with the stallion Svadilfari. Loki is actually the mother of Odin's eight legged horse.

Heimdall

- Guardian of the Bifrost Bridge
- Watchman of the gods
- He is able to hear the grass grow on the hillside and the wool on a sheep's back
- He can see a hundred miles by day or night
- He requires less sleep than a bird
- Described as being very white with golden hair and golden eyes with golden teeth.
- His nickname if Gullintani

- He is also known as Rig or Riger, the divine sire of the various classes of the human race.
- Odin — Father
- Nine Wave Maidens — Mother
- Hnoss — Close companion
- Himinbiorg — Palace
- Gulltop — Horse
- Giallarhorn — Trumpet
- Hofud — Sword

Vidar

- God of imperishable matter
- Symbol of resurrection and renewal
- Described as the strong silent type
- The personification of the imperishable forces of Nature
- Depicted as tall, well built and handsome.
- Wears a great leather soled shoe
- Destined to avenge his father at Ragnarok
- Odin — Father
- Grid — Mother
- Landvidi — The land where his place sits

Aegir

- God of the sea
- He causes and then calms tempests

- Described as a gaunt old man with long white hair and scraggly white beard. He has claw-like fingers that are always convulsively clutching the air.
- Kari   Brother
- Loki   Brother
- Ran   Sister/Wife
- Gialp   Daughter with Ran
- Augeida   Daughter with Ran
- Sindur   Daughter with Ran
- Greip   Daughter with Ran
- Ulfrun   Daughter with Ran
- Atla   Daughter with Ran
- Egia   Daughter with Ran
- Aurgiafa   Daughter with Ran
- Iarnsaxa   Daughter with Ran
- Elde   Servant
- Funfeng   Servant
- Hlesey   Land where his place sits

Hoenir

- Called the Bright One
- Gave motion and senses to mankind
- Reserved, tall, & handsome with long legs and a swift gait.
- Odin   Brother

Hermod

- Messenger of the gods

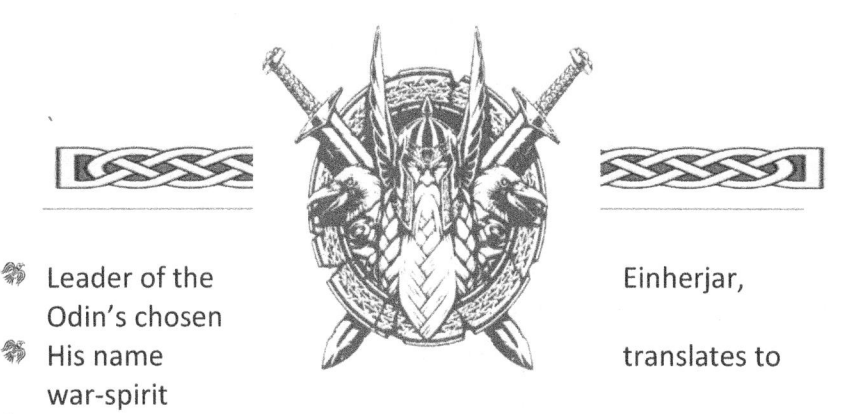

- Leader of the Einherjar, Odin's chosen
- His name translates to war-spirit
- Bright and beautiful, gifted with great speed
- Blond hair, beard with blue eyes
- Often accompanies the Valkyries
- Odin   Father
- Frigga   Mother
- Balder   Brother
- Hodur   Brother
- Gambantein   Magical staff

Odur

- Symbol of the summer sun
- The wandering god
- Regarded as an emblem of passion or of the intoxicating pleasures of love
- Freyja   Wife
- Hnoss   Daughter with Freyja
- Gersemi   Daughter with Freyja

Tyr

- God of martial honor, courage, victory and sacrifice.
- Only has one hand

- Short brown hair and beard. Dark eyes that look deeply into a person or situation. Wears dark clothing
- Has no palace of his own, stays in Valhalla

VALKYRIES
By Kristoffer Alric Allison

Where there is fighting, and brave men fall

There will be rejoicing in Odin's hall.

Battle maidens pick up sword and spears

As ravens whisper into Odin's ears.

He holds gungnir aloft to point the way

As Valkyries charge out on steeds of gray.

The song of battle calls the choosers of the slain

As weapons clang and men scream in pain.

Look to the sky and embrace them as they near,

Listen to the thunder as the warriors of Valhalla cheer.

The Valkyries are the "choosers of the slain." They are the adopted daughters of Odin and appear as the beautiful warrior-maidens on winged horses, armed with helmets, armor and spears. Their purpose is to visit battlefields and choose the most heroic of those who have died in battle (called Einherjar) and carry them off to the halls Valhalla and Folkvang.

Those warriors will be those who accompany Odin and fight by his side at the preordained battle at the end of the world, Ragnarok.

Originally, Valkyries were frightful battle-spirits accompanying Odin in his work of marking men for death in war. They appear in a more pleasant aspect in Valhalla, where they carry out the traditional womanly duty of bearing drink to the Einherjar.

The Valkyries protect Odin's heroes through life and choose amongst the dead who goes to Valhalla. They serve as purveyors of wisdom, protection, and at death help the fallen hero make the difficult journey to Valhalla.

The Valkyries are often associated with the Norns, this may be due to their role at death. In myth, they have been seen as both very fierce ugly hags relishing in bloodshed and as beautiful young women living to serve the hero to which they are assigned. Both aspects are most likely true. The former view goes back to an earlier time when they were seen, like their god, as beings of rage and wind, the fury of battle. However, this does not stop them from taking on other aspects which are gentler.

The Valkyries also acted as Odin's messengers. Their armor, which shone while doing his bidding, was once thought to have caused Aurora Borealis.

List of Valkyries

Name	Meaning
Brunhilde	Bright Battle
Geirolul	Spear waver
Goll	Tumult
Gondul	Wand wielder
Gudrun	Battle Rune
Gunn	War
Herfjoturr	Host fetter
Hildr	Battle
Hlokk	Noise
Hrist	Shaker
Mist	Cloud
Randgrid	Shield truce
Radgrid	Council truce
Reginleif	Power trace
Skeggjold	Axe age
Skogul	Shaker
Skuld	Debt
Sigrdrifa	Victory urge
Sigrun	Victory Rune
Svafa	Sleep maker
Thrima	Fight

Other Divine/Semi-Divine Beings

     There are other entities or beings that are considered divine, or semi-divine beings within the context of the Heathen religion. Some of these beings were given honor to or "worshipped" and others were not, according to many historical or linguistic records.

     Regardless, they are important in the overall system of belief in that they give us keys into many of the symbols and mystical spiritualism that encompass our world. Some are what one may call malevolent towards mankind and to the tribes of gods, others neutral, and others are beneficial towards the realms and aims of the Aesir and Vanir.

Giants

After Audhumla, the cosmic cow, the giants were the first creatures that came to life in the vast expanse called Ginnungagap
. These giants and their descendents have always been the personification of the harshness and inhospitable side of nature and the chaotic forces that have made life difficult for gods and man alike. So, it is no surprise that from that the very beginning, giants have been the opponents and the enemies of the gods who were born of the same cosmic maelstrom yet evolved to travel down a more structured and enlightened path.

As the separation and the animosity grew between the giants and the gods, it inevitably came to blows. Odin and his two brothers Vili and Ve slew the first giant, Ymir. As he fell lifeless, his children and grandchildren were drowned by a tidal wave of blood that poured out from his body. Only two survived; Bergelmir and his wife. They fled to the world of Jotunheim, where they claimed the rough, uncivilized world as their own, and became the ancestors for all the giants that came after. Having become the parents of all the giants that came after, they are the original giant ancestors.

Here is a list of giants currently known to me. I have listed the males first and then the females. The lists are separate to aid in understanding. There are others who are not yet known, but they will be.

Male Giants

Name	Meaning
Alfarin	The far-traveled
Alsvartr	The completely black one
Alsvidr	The completely white one
Alvaldi	The powerful one
Amr	The dark one
Aurgelmir	The roarer
Aurgrimnir	The angry one
Aurnir	
Beinvidr	
Beli	Bellower
Bergelmir	The mountain-bellower
Bjorgolfr	Mountain-wolf
Blapthvari	Chatter pole
Brandingi	The burning one
Brimir	
Dofri	The lazy one
Dumbr	The stupid one
Durnir	The sleeper
Eggther	One with the bodyguards
Eimgeitir	The steaming
Eimnir	Burner
Eldr	Fire
Fjolsvidr	Much knower
Fjolverkr	The one who works a lot

Fleggr	Monster
Galarr	Screamer
Gangr	
Gait	
Geirrodr	Protected from spears
Geitr	The goat herder
Gillingr	The noisy one
Glamar	Pale one
Glaumarr	Noisy one
Grimlingr	The masked little one
Grimnir	The masked one
Gripnir	
Grasper	
Gusir	The stormy one
Gyllir	The shouting one
Gymir	Sea
Hadda	Hairy
Hafli	The greedy one
Hardgreipr	Hard grasper
Hardverkr	Hard worker
Hastigi	High climber
Heidr	Heath
Herkir	Noisy one
Hlebardr	Wolf-bear
Hloi	Roarer
Hraudnir	Destroyer
Hraudungr	Destroyer
Hrimgrimnir	Frost-grimnir
Hrimnir	Frost covered

Hringvolnir	Staff with ring
Hripstodr	
Hroarr	
Hrokkvir	The bent one
Hrolfr	
Hrossthjofr	Horse thief
Hrungnir	Brawler
Hrymr	
Idi	Moveable
Imr	Dark one
Jokull	Glacier
Kaldgrani	Cold beard
Kari	Wind
Kottr	Cat
Kyrmir	Pusher
Leidi	The hated
Leifi	Heir
Logi	Fire
Lutr	Stooped over
Midi	Middle
Midjungr	Middle being
Mogthrasir	
Nati	
Olvaldi	The beer keeper
Ondudr	The terrible
Ornir	Rock
Osgrui	Heap of ashes
Oskrudr	Bellower
Ofoti	The legless

Ogladnir	The cheerless
Rangbeinn	Crooked leg
Saekarlsmuli	Shark mouth
Salfangr	
Samendill	
Skaerir	Shearer
Skalli	Bald headed
Skerkir	Noise maker
Skrati	Troll
Skrymir	Boaster
Somr	
Sprettingr	Jumper
Starkadr	
Stigandi	Climber
Stumi	Stumbler
Surtr	The black one
Suttungr	Heavy with drink
Svadi	Careless
Svarangr	Clumsy one
Svarthofdi	Blackhead
Svartr	Black one
Thistilbardi	Thistle-beard
Thiassi	
Thrigeitir	
Thrivaldi	Very mighty
Thrudgelmir	Powerful shouter
Thurbord	Dried out cheeks
Vafthrudnir	Mighty entangler
Vagnhofdi	Whale-head

Vandill
Vidblindi   Very blind
Vidgripr   Far grasper
Vindr   Wind
Vindsvalr   Cold wind
Viparr   Bristly one
Vornir   Careful
Ymir

Giantesses

Ama   The dark one
Amgerdr   Dark Gerdr
Angrboda   The bringer of grief
Atla   Argumentative one
Bakrauf   Backside
Bestla   Bark
Bryja   Troll woman
Buseyra   Big ears
Drifa   Flurry of snow
Drofn   Wave
Eisurfala   Ash-troll
Fala   Fool
Fenja   Worker
Fjolvor   The careful one
Fonn   Snowdrift
Forad   Danger
Geitla   The little goat
Gestilia   Guest

Geysa	The cheeky one
Glumra	Noisy one
Gneip	Peak
Gneypa	The bent one
Gnissa	Grating one
Goi	Wintry
Greip	Grasp
Gridr	Greedy
Grima	Mask
Grisla	Piglet
Grottintanna	Gaping teeth
Gryla	Troll woman
Guma	
Gunnlod	Invitation to battle
Haera	The grey-haired one
Hala	Hide
Hardgreip	Hard Grabber
Hengjankjapta	Hanging chin
Herkja	Noisy woman
Hildr	
Hrimgardr	Frost gerder
Hryga	Heap
Hrygoa	Sorrowful one
Hyndla	Lap dog
Hyrrokkin	Withered by fire
Ima	Dusty one
Imgerdr	
Jarnglumra	Iron roarer
Jarnsaxa	Iron knife

Jarnvithja	From the Iron Forest
Keila	Gorge
Kjallandi	
Kraka	Crow
Leikn	Bewitched
Leirvor	Dirty-lipped
Ljota	Ugly
Lothinfingra	Shaggy finger
Margerdr	Sea-gerder
Menja	Slave girl
Mjoll	Powdered snow
Morn	The grinding one
Munnharpa	Shriveled mouth
Munnrida	Chatterbox
Myrkrida	Dark rider
Oflugbarda	Strong beard
Rifingafla	Forked gable
Rygr	Woman
Simul	Female Reindeer
Sivor	Drooping lips
Skrikja	Screamer
Svara	Heavy one
Sveipinfalda	Hidden in a hood
Thokk	Joy
Unngerdr	Wave gerder
Vardrun	Guard rune
Vigglod	Happy in battle

Dwarfs

Odin and his two brothers had slain the mighty giant Ymir. As they pondered over what to do with his enormous remains, the body began to rot, and creatures began to form. Over time they became small homely looking beings, and Odin took notice of their large heads and short limbs. The other gods began to notice them as well, and although they were less powerful than the gods, they were shrewd, cunning and full of guile. This craftiness gave them the ability to collect knowledge and use it to their advantage. This prompted Odin to give them the world known as Svartalfaheim. There they dug down into the rocky underworld to make their home.

They hid away from the sunlight. If a single ray of the flaming orb touches their skin, they turn into stone. Using their calculating intelligence, they turned their underground domain to their advantage though. They have learned to mine for gold and silver and how to hunt down precious jewels. They have become the best of smiths, the creators of glorious jewelry and powerful weapons. Some of their creations have been gifted to the gods, while others have been inherited by the heroes of mankind. We provide you a list of their names, just so they are remembered.

Name	**Meaning**
Ai	Ancestor
Alf	Elf

Alfrigg	Experienced one
Althiofer	The perfect thief
Alvis	Omniscient
An	Distinguished friend
Anarr	The other one
Andvari	The careful one
Atvarder	The defender
Aurvarger	Gravel-wolf
Austri	East
Barri	Fool
Berlinger	Short beam
Bifurr	The quaking one
Blder	Knife
Billinger	Hermaphrodite
Blainn	Black
Blavorr	Shining one
Bindvider	Hidden tree
Bomburr	Fatty
Brisinger	Flame
Brokker	Blacksmith
Bruni	Brown one
Buinn	Ever-ready
Buri	Inhabitant
Burinn	Son of
Dagfinner	Day-finder
Dainn	Died
Dellinger	The shining one
Dorri	Spear-fighter
Dolger	Enemy

Dolgthrasir	The hostile one
Dori	The damager
Draupnir	Goldsmith
Dufr	Sleepy-one
Dulinn	The hidden one
Durinn	Door-keeper
Durnir	The sleeper
Dvalinn	The slow one
Eggmoin	Killed by sword
Eikinskialdi shield	The one with oaken
Eitri	Poisonous one
Fainn	The colored one
Faler	Hider
Far	Danger
Farli	Traveler
Fider	Magician
Fili	File
Fialarr	Deceiver
Fiolsvider	Very wise one
Fornbogi	The old bow
Forve	Forge
Fraeger	Famous one
Frar	The quick one
Fror	Nimble
Frosti	Frost
Fullanger	Lazy smell
Fundinn	The found one
Galarr	Screamer

Gandalfer	Magic worker
Ginnar	Deceiver
Gloi	Glowing one
Grerr	The small one
Grimer	Masked one
Gullmaevill	Little golden seagull
Guster	Gust
Haenbui	Tree
Hanarr	Skillful
Harr	The grey one
Haugspori	Hill-treader
Hepti	Grasp
Heri	Hare
Hildinger	Warrior
Hlediolfer	Protective wolf
Hlevanger	Filed wolf
Hliodolfer	Howling wolf
Hogstari	Witty
Hugstari	Stubborn one
Ingi	
Iri	The rumor spreading
Jaki	Icicle
Jari	Quarrelsome
Kili	Wedge
Lithskialfer	Limb dangler
Liter	Colored one
Liomi	Splendor
Lofarr	Praiser
Loinn	Lazy

Loni	
Midvider	Middle board
Miodvitnir	Mead wolf
Mioklituder	The strongly colored
Modsognir	Tired one
Modvitnir	Angry wolf
Muninn	Memory
Nabbi	Bump
Naefer	Capable
Nali	Needle
Narr	Fool
Nefi	Nephew
Nidi	Dark one
Nipinger	Sorrowful
Nordri	North
Nori	Little piece
Nyi	New
Nyrader	New advisor
Onn	Work
Oinn	Fearless
Onarr	
Ori	Mannish one
Orinn	The quarrelsome
Radspaker	Quick-witted
Radvider	Giver of wise advice
Rekker	Warrior
Sindri	Blacksmith
Skavaerr	Crooked one
Skavidr	Slanting tree

Skirvir	Spitter
Solblindi	Sun-blind
Sudri	South
Sviurr	Vanishing one
Thekker	
Thiodroerir	Bellower
Thiorr	Bull
Thorinn	Brave one
Thrainn	Threatening one
Thrar	Stubborn
Thrasir	Furious
Throinn	Growing
Thror	Thriving
Thulinn	Murmurer
Tigvae	
Toki	Fool
Uri	The smith
Varr	The careful one
Vegdrasill	Way-horse
Vegger	Wedge
Veiger	Drinker
Vestri	West
Vider	Tree
Vili	Will
Vindalfer	Bent dwarf
Virvir	Dyer
Viter	Wise
Yngvi	Prince or warrior

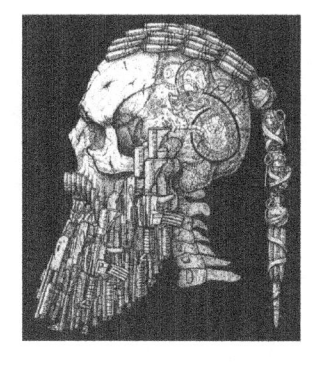

Guards

- Alberich — Dwarven King, powerful magician, guards the Nibelung hoard.
- Fafnir — Worm that guards the treasure of light
- Garm — Giant hound who guards the entrance to Helheim
- Surt — Guards the world of fire
- Ginnungagap — The gap separating Niflheim and Muspell
- Svalin — The shield that protects the worlds from the full power of the sun

Halls and Locations

- Bilskirnir — Thor's hall
- Breidablik — Balder's place
- Brunnaker — Where Idunna's apple grove is located
- Cattegat — The place where Aegir dwells
- Elvidner — Hel's palace
- Eubea — Aegir's hall
- Fensalir — Frigga's palace
- Folkvang — Freyja's realm
- Gladsheim — Council hall of the gods
- Glitnir — Forseti's hall
- Himinbiorg — Heimdall's palace
- Noatun — Njord's home
- Sessrymnir — Freyja's palace
- Sokkvabekk — Saga's palace
- Thrudheim — Thor's realm
- Valaskialf — A hall in Asgard
- Vigrid — The plain where the final will be fought
- Valhalla — Odin's hall where the warriors who fall in battle go after death
- Ydalir — Uller's dwelling place

Animals

- Alsvider — Horse who pulls the moon chariot
- Alsvin — Horse who pulls the sun chariot
- Arvakr — Horse who pulls the sun chariot
- Audhumla — The cosmic cow who nourished Ymir
- Blodughofi — Frey's horse
- Dain — Stag who eats the leaves of Yggdrasil
- Duneyr — Stag who feeds on the leaves of Yggdrasil
- Durathor — Stag who feeds on the leaves of Yggdrasil
- Dvlainn — Stag who feeds on the leaves of Yggdrasil
- Fenris — Wolf, son of Loki and Kills Odin at Ragnarok
- Freki — One of Odin's wolves
- Garm — Guardian dog of Hel
- Geri — One of Odin's wolves
- Gulltop — Heimdall's horse
- Gullfaxi — Hrungnir's horse
- Gullinbursti — Frey's golden boar

- Gullinkambi — Rooster of Midgard who will sound the alarm when Ragnarok begins.
- Hati — Wolf who pursues the moon
- Heidrun — Goat who supplies mead to warriors in Valhalla
- Hofvarpnir — Gna's swift running horse
- Hraesvelgr — Eagle that causes the wind to Blow
- Hrimfaxi — Horse who draws the night across the sky
- Hugin — One of Odin's ravens
- Iormungandr — Loki's child, world serpent
- Munin — One of Odin's ravens
- Nidhogg — Serpent who gnaws Yggdrasil's roots
- Ratatosk — Squirrel that runs up and down Yggdrasil spreading discontent between the eagle above and the serpent below
- Saehrimnir — Boar who provides the meat to warriors in Valhalla
- Skinfaxi — Horse that brings day to the sky
- Skoll — Wolf who pursues the sun in an attempt to devour it
- Sleipnir — Odin's eight-legged horse
- Svadilfare — Horse who fathered Sleipnir and helped the giant build the wall around Asgard
- Tanngniostr — One of Thor's goats
- Tanngrisnir — One of Thor's goats

The Jotuns

"Jotun" in its modern usage is a general term for the giant-kind whom are descended from Ymir. They symbolically and mystically embody the forces of the universe before the coming of the gods and are generally the chaotic forces of nature in its severest shapes.

The Jotuns can be categorized further into three classes according to their general nature. These classes are Rises, Jotuns, and Thurses.

The **Rises** are stereotypical types of giants which are thought of as being of great size and engendered themselves with humans and other entities. They are not very intelligent, slothful, and beneficial to mankind on a one-on-one basis. They dwell in parts of mountains and rocky hills. An example would be the not-so-bright giants of folklore who sometimes befriend children in various tales or are the bad guys who are outwitted by the youngsters.

The **Jotuns** are non-evolving entities who are ancient, wise, intelligent, and are neutral entities in the war between consciousness and unconsciousness, symbolically. Some Jotuns side with the Aesir and Vanir, while others side with the Thurses. They have acted the same way throughout time. Some examples of Etins would be Mímir, Skadi, Thiassi, and Thrym. Mímir and are beneficial to the goals of the gods. Jotuns of a beneficial nature are commonly taken as mates by the gods. Thiassi, and Thrym, are examples of Jotuns who are against the Aesir and Vanir.

The **Thurses** are immensely powerful, insanely violent, non-intelligent, and relatively non-thinking beings in the multiverse. They are the antagonists and enemies of the gods and that of existence itself.

Two sub-divisions of the Thurses exist: **Rime-Thurses** and **Fire-Thurses**. The Rime-Thurses are of the essences of chaotic ice and the Fire-Thurses of the essences of chaotic fire. These beings are never worshipped. They are the devourers of all life and seek only to destroy. A perfect example of a Fire-Thurse would be Surtr "the Black (or Scorched) One" who is prophesied to lead the sons of Muspellheim to enflame the multiverse and destroy all.

The Tomten

The Tomten is a type of house-ghost or house-wight whose name means roughly, "homestead man". They are similar to the Norwegian Napfhans and the Kobolds of Germany. Known by other names such as Gardvord ("farm guardian"), and Tunkall ("yard fellow"), they associate themselves with either a home itself or a specific family that catches their fancy.

A happy Tomte will help with the housework, guard/protect the home, and bring luck to the family. An unhappy Tomten will hide objects and play tricks. One of the most important times to give attention to a Tomte of the home is during Yuletide, in which they expect to receive a bowl of porridge or oatmeal with a good-sized pad of butter.

The oldest literary reference, given by Reimund Kvideland and Henning Sehmsdorf, to the farm sprite is found in a version of the Saga of Olaf Tryggvasson (twelfth century), in which one is referred to as Armaður ("hearth man").

Landvaetr/Landwights

Landvaetr is actually the more accurate name but it has begun to fall out of usage and Landwights has taken its place. Either way, the names mean land spirits.

Landwights come from the traditions of Northern Europe where they believe that there are powerful spirits that dwell among the roots, rocks, waterfalls, fields, ponds and streams. Even to this day their presence is felt and honored by those who choose to pay attention.

These spirits are so important to the people of Scandinavia that they once held up the construction of an important airport for two weeks. They believed that there were Landwights living within a large boulder and thought that the two weeks would give them enough time to relocate.

Offending Landwights is no small matter. It is said that an angry Wight may bring about infertile lands along with hardships for people in the surrounding area. They can create uncomfortable feelings and cause conflict to arise between partners. That is why you should leave out gifts or treats for the Landwights where you live. They will bring balance and harmony when they are honored and respected.

If you truly want to connect to the Landwights or Nature Spirits in your area then offer them food and drink. The best food offerings are always in their natural state: fruits, nuts, seeds or raw vegetables. Always use something that you know won't harm the local animals who may sneak a nibble. Drink offerings can be a little more varied; you can use milk, juices, wine, beer, ale or mead. Try to confine it to liquids that won't harm the vegetation. Remember, you want to be giving something, not taking something away. Another great way to do more of an intimate bonding is to sit in their presence quietly contemplating or meditating. You could also sing a song, read a poem or even tell a story. It is your good will and respect that will bring the Landwights to your side. If you can manage to build a bond or at least ensure that they are content then they will bless and aid you for years to come. They are thought to be living embodiments of various features of the natural world. They may also be the spirits of people who have died in that particular place or were alive and have returned to protect it.

No matter whether the Landwights are living embodiments of nature or returned spirits; the land and those who dwell upon it depends upon their strength and happiness. If they are weak, frightened or angry, then the land will not thrive and the people who live upon it will not prosper.

Pay attention to them. Make offerings to them and include them in holiday celebrations as well as everyday events. Your land will thrive and so will your family's health and well-being. You will feel their happiness as it infects everything and everyone around you.

Symbols

These symbols pre-date much farther than many realize. These symbols are not runes. Runes are entirely different in their content, meaning, and context. These are the major, and most common, symbols within the Heathen religion. There are many more which one can find through searching archeological digs and other academic studies.

The Hammer of Thor otherwise known as Mjollnir, is the ultimate symbol of warding and protection. Most of the Heathen folk wear a representation of the hammer. In elder days, during the conversions of Christianity, folks wore the hammer, instead of the cross, to show their loyalty as it is today in the modern era.

The Sun-wheel is a symbol that corresponds with the holy year, and the sun's power of weal. It is one of the oldest known Northern European solar symbols.

Vaulknot, or "knot of the slain", is a symbol of the cult of Odin. It signifies the god's power to fetter and unfetter the soul, the workings of wyrd, and orlog. The vaulknot can also symbolize the 3 levels of self-evolution and dozens of other things. The realm of the symbology of the vaulknot is immense.

The Triskelion, is a symbol of the three-fold pattern of the realms of being. This encompasses the realms of Asgard, Midgard, and Hel. It may also be representative of the evolution of man in the Rígsþula of the Poetic Edda. Many Heathen folk associate this symbol with the god, Heimdall.

The Irminsûl is a symbol of the great pillar axis of the worlds, according to Saxon lore, with its apex at the North Star. It was also a symbol of cosmic order. Originally linked to an Old Saxon god, Irmin, in modern times, it has been associated as being a symbol of Tyr among the Heathen.

The Aegishjalmar, or "Helm of Awe", is a magical symbol which is still used in Icelandic magic. Its power is to cause paralyzing fear in the hearts of your enemies. Mentioned in the Volsunga Saga, the wyrm, Fafnir possessed it until it was defeated by Sigurd.

The Shield-Knot is a strong symbol of protection that is still used today to mark off archeological digs and historical cultural sites in Scandinavia.

Ritual Regalia

There are certain tools that are used for rituals within Heathen religions. They are usually symbolic of larger more divine items that help observers focus on the event at hand as well as setting the necessary mood. Most of the items are used during the course of a blot but can also be incorporated into a more elaborate sumble. If certain items are not available then you can use substitutes that will function for the intended purpose. You don't have to be elaborate; the gods are more concerned with your intent than the tools you use.

The Harrow- A harrow, or altar, is traditionally kept outside and was made up of stone or heaped stones.

The Hammer- A hammer is used as a representation of the holy hammer of Thor, Mjollnir. Representing the primal powers of both primordial fire & primordial ice, it is used in hallowing and blessing objects and sometimes people.

The Drinking Horn- The drinking horn is used to consume the holy mead, ale, or beer used in ritual. The horn becomes a symbol of the Well of Wyrd when in use. When drinking from, or kissing the side of, the horn one is consuming or sharing in the power that the gods have instilled within the liquid.

The Hlautbolli- The Hlautbolli or blot-bowl, is used to catch blood from a sacrifice, or to contain mead from a sumble until it is poured upon the earth or a harrow. It should be made out of a natural material such as wood or stone.

The Hlautteinar-The hlautteinar are the sacrificial twigs or aspergills which are used to sprinkle the hlaut (sacrificial blood) onto blessed items or people. Usually it is made from freshly cut pine/coniferous tree branches.

The Oath Ring- An oath ring is used to declare or swear oaths upon a most serious nature.

`The Glóðker- A glóðker is a small firepot used to burn incense or to keep a small need-fire, or a flame via flammable liquid. It is symbolic of the original flames of creation and the flame of the souls of our ancestors.

The Sax- The sax, or scram sax, is the sacrificial knife used for literal blot of an animal. It can also be utilized for runic carving purposes.

The Gandr Staff- A staff engraved with runes and knot-work.

The Calendar

Monday	Moon's Day
Tuesday	Tiu's Day *
Wednesday	Woden Day
Thursday	Thor's Day
Friday	Frigg's Day #
Saturday	Saturn's Day
Sunday	Day of the Sun

*After the Germanic god of war, also known as Tyr
#Frigg was the wife of Odin, also known as Woden.

January	Snowmoon
February	Horning
March	Lenting
April	Summer Finding
May	Merrymoon
June	Midyear
July	Haymoon
August	Harvest
September	Shedding
October	Hunting
November	Fogmoon
December	Yulemoon

Holidays and Celebrations

January/Snowmoon 14 -- Thorrablot

On this day we celebrate Thor as he battles against the frost giants that threaten Midgard.

This is a celebration that has its roots firmly planted within the Viking age. For Heathens it is a time to celebrate and honor Thor; the Defender of Asgard, Guardian of Midgard, and the Breaker of Winter's back.

Thorrablot, also known as Thor's feast is observed with parties, physical competitions and a feast. This is when we pay tribute and make sacrifices to Thor as he does battle with the Frost giants.

On this day we come together to eat, drink and be merry, Thor's favorite past times. As we stay indoors close to the warm fires, it is a great time to tell your favorite stories of the gods. Thorrablot takes place during the coldest days of the year, when a warm meal, strong mead, close friends and family are all necessary to warm the spirit. After feasting, or while feasting, it's time for games, songs, dancing, stories and let's keep that mead flowing!

Embrace those close to you, build the fires higher and don't forget to honor Thor. Toast him and tip back an extra horn of mead. Without his epic battles and constant victories against the icy encroach of the frost giants there would be no spring to look forward to.

There are many ways to celebrate Thor's blot. From a sacrifice of mead and boar's meat to a few healthy toasts from your drinking horn followed by a hearty hail! Give thanks to the mightiest Son of Odin, Wielder of the hammer, Miollnir, god of Storms, and Defender of Asgard. Make a sacrifice and make a toast.

February/ Horning 2 -- Charming of the Plow

This day represents Frey's wooing of Gerd. Frey's heated passion can be seen as the sun thawing the cold shoulder that the giantess Gerd first gave him. It is a festival of fertility so Frey is also the personification of fertility, while Gerd represents the earth.

This day is the symbolic wooing by Frey of the giantess Gerd. Frey represents fertility and Gerd is the personification of the frozen earth. It is an ancient belief that our ancestors actually learned to plow the earth from watching wild boar digging their tusks into the soil. Our astute ancestors realized that the freshly churned up soil produced greener and lusher vegetation than the undisturbed dirt. You may well remember that Frey does indeed own a boar.

This is a festival of fertility, a time to put seeds into the tilled up earth. I will refrain from winking and pointing back to Frey and his new wife Gerd.

New seeds being planted are also symbolic of new beginnings.

The harshness of winter is coming to an end, and although our lives are much different than what our ancestors lived through, it is a time to remember their struggles. Envision their hopes and their dreams that were inspired by this festival. Always look ahead, always plant the seeds of your future success.

This is the day when we honor all beings that have to do with fertility and the approaching spring. Celebrate Frey, Freyja, Frigga, Sif, Nerthus, Ostara and Jord. Pay tribute to the spirits of the land and give thanks for the gifts that they give us. A gift for a gift.

This is when we prepare for the planting season. The plow is blessed, even if it is only a symbolic plow; then the first furrow is dug. This furrow is filled with offerings for a productive season. This plow is a powerful symbol, it demonstrates our willful penetration of the hard and unyielding soil. Things don't just happen. We inflict our will upon life, and we make things happen.

Celebrate and have a great time, but plant the seeds today of whatever you wish to harvest in the future. Success and productivity are not hoped for, they are planned for!

March/Lenting 21 -- Summer Finding

This is the Spring Equinox; the end of winter and the beginning of the season of rebirth. This is the time that we honor Idunna, Frigga, Freyja, and Nerthus. This is a celebration of nature as it makes its return.

This holiday is celebrated on the Spring Equinox which falls on or near this date. The celebration marks the beginning of the warmer parts of the year. Humans, animals, and plants fill up with the vigorousness that the season brings.

It's our time to celebrate the rejuvenation of the earth, fertility and growth. Traditional decorations include budding boughs, flowers, colored eggs joined together with a rabbit motif. This is the time when the mating season begins, especially for birds and rabbits. During this time of the year, you can find male hares jumping around wildly and acting crazy. This is where the phrase "crazy as a March hare" originates.

Heathen customs associated with the celebration of Summer Finding include children dancing around an alter dedicated to Idunna, decorating it with white flowers. There is also the decorating and coloring of eggs which were brought by the eastern hare. The adults then hide and the children seek out the delicious treats. A great way to add to the festivities is by baking cakes and cookies in the shape of rabbits, but ask Idunna for her blessings before sharing with your guests.

Another great tradition is the performance of plays, or the reading of poems wherein warmth battles against the cold of the northern realms. Be creative, it is the time to celebrate life. Winter is behind us and the warmth is here.

Summer Finding is a celebration of the awakening earth, the gods and goddesses, the human soul, and nature's lust for life. Everything becomes brighter, more joyful and more productive after the Summer Finding feast. Enjoy, and celebrate the goddesses in all her springtime glory.

May/Merrymoon 1 -- May Day

The fields are greener and the meadows are decorated with colorful flowers. This is a day to give thanks to Freyja for all the gifts that she bestows upon us.

This is the equivalent of a heathen Valentine's Day. It is meant to be a night of courtship and love; done in our own unique way. Young men are expected to go out and gather fresh green branches and colorful flowers; which they are expected to use to decorate the windows of the young ladies they're interested in. Freyja, as the goddess of love and desire is definitely the sponsor of this particular festival.

One of the main traditional events is the raising of a large maypole, or the decorating of a May tree, that is centrally located and designated for this purpose. No matter whether it is a pole or a tree, it is an ancient symbol of this fertility ritual. Around this site there should be room for bonfires, dancing, and outdoor feasting.

Fires are used to light up the night, and it's even customary to leap through the flames for luck.

It is a time to celebrate the maturity of the earth and the next generation as they take their steps into adulthood. Plants are reaching their full growth during this time of year, and it is time for us to recognize that our young are doing the same.

Look to Freyja as she makes her presence felt in the twinkling of eyes and flirtatious winks. Toast her loudly and joyfully, it is a time for bonfires, happiness and romance!

Drink, dance, feast, drink, dance, and feast some more! Make your deepest love know that they are deeply loved!

June/Midyear 21 -- Midsummer

This is the longest day and the shortest night of the year. Sol begins her long decline into the darkness which culminates during Yule. This is when we celebrate the brightness and beauty of Balder. This was also the traditional date when the All-thing was held.

This was once one of the widest spread of holidays and has always been held on the Summer Solstice. Its traditions and celebrations used to be found throughout all the countries of Northern Europe, and even now they are making a huge comeback.

The Summer Solstice has the longest day of the year with the shortest night. This is a night for roaring bonfires, speeches, songs, dancing, drinking and feasting. Traditions include the making of wreaths, the kindling of fires, and the burning of corn dollies, which are little human figures made of straw.

Midsummer is the time to make offerings to Balder. Small ships are often made and then filled with offerings before they are set on fire. This is the high point of the year; the time when great deeds are accomplished and when the heart is filled with daring. Our ancestors considered this to be raiding season; the crops were planted, winds filled the sails and distant shores beckoned with unconquered lands, and rich spoils. It is the season of action and for risk taking; it is time to reach for your goals without fear.

It's time for us to recognize the death of the fair god of sunshine, Balder, along with his beautiful and devoted wife, Nanna. Summer has reached its highest point, and the sun shines longer today than at any other time of the year. After today's celebrations and offerings the days will begin to shorten as the earth begins its slow descent into winter and darkness. A seasonal Ragnarok as the ice giants approach, but it is with a promise of Balder's return to rewarm us.

August/Harvest 19 -- Freyfaxi

This is a celebration of the harvest; it's a time to feast on seasonal fruits and grains while making offerings to Frey. This was the traditional time to harvest the crops, and this is when we celebrate the first fruits of that harvest. Heathens celebrate this holiday by baking figures of the god Frey and his boar into bread and cookies. Remember the holiday "Charming of the Plow" that took place earlier in the year? This holiday is the result of that hard work, sacrifice, and tribute that we invested. Everything in nature is about cycles.

This is when we take in the first fruits of the harvest season and it is customary to donate something to those who are in need. The first parts of the harvest are blessed and offered to the gods; just as the last part of the harvest is left in the field as a dedication to the gods.

We feast and honor Frey as the god of fertility; Thor as god of the harvest, and his wife Sif, whose long golden hair is the symbol of fields of ripened grain.

This is the end of summer and the beginning of the hard work that is necessary as we prepare for winter. We are celebrating all of our hard work and the bountiful harvest that came from our efforts. We are also giving back to the gods for what they have provided us through nature, and for the lessons that we have learned. Make sure to include in your feasting breads, seasonal fruit and vegetables.

Most of us are not farmers, and hence don't grow our own crops or do our own harvesting, but we still depend upon the land for our nourishment. The earth and the harvest sustain us; even if we go to the grocery store rather than the field.

We honor Frey because he fertilizes the fields and enriches the soil so that the plants grow and flourish. We give thanks to Thor for the life sustaining rain that he brings with his storms. We pay tribute to Sif, for it is her golden colored hair that let us know when the grains have ripened.

This holiday is ancient and was felt way more intimately by our ancestors because their literal survival depended upon harvests. Look to the past; without the sustenance that they themselves gathered from the earth, and the fertile fields, they may not have made it. If just one of your ancestors hadn't survived then you wouldn't be here. Give thanks to Frey for his fertility of the earth and our ancestral wombs. Go out and plant a tree, a bush, or plant. Give back to the earth that gives you so much, and remember that trees and plants provide oxygen; it is always a gift for a gift.

September/Shedding 21 -- Winter Finding

The Autumn Equinox; summer and winter are in a state of balance for a brief time, but the cold and darkness are fast approaching. Prepare for chillier temperatures and longer nights as you feast and make sacrifices to Odin.

This is the Autumn Equinox, the beginning of fall. This particular celebration is known by several different names: Winter Finding, Fall Feast, and Haustblot, but no matter the name we know that our people have celebrated this time of year for as long as we can trace our history.

Practically speaking, this is the season when our people collected and stored food for the long winter ahead. They prepared their homes for the coming ice, wind and snow while bringing the livestock into their winter quarters. Remember, this struggle for survival and the hardships that your family once endured, but also the strength that it took to endure them. Raise a horn and toast their incredible fortitude.

Bonfires, feasting, dancing and socializing played a large part in the festivities. Our people would never willingly let an opportunity pass by if it gave us a reason to party and to be with our loved ones. They would build up a huge central bonfire and when it was blazing so brightly that it chased away the darkness, they'd run around putting out every other fire in the village. Each family would then light their hearth fires from the central flame, bonding all of the families together and reminding them that they relied upon and were connected to each other.

This is a time to gather, feast, reflect on life and give thanks for what you have. It is a time to celebrate life as you pay tribute to the wheel of nature and the rhythm of life as it heads toward the season of death. It is a cycle; death and decay nurtures and brings forth new life.

October/Hunting 31 -- Winter Nights

This is a time of reflection as we celebrate the last true harvest of the year. We enjoy the bounties that we've collected; pay tribute to Freyja and honor the Disir.

The summer seasons have now made a definite turn toward winter. There is no turning back; it is time for us to focus our attention on the inside.

This is the final harvest of the year. It is the time when our distant kin would butcher the livestock that they didn't expect to live through the colder months; this would provide families with enough meat to last the winter, while insuring that the remaining livestock would be fed without suffering starvation.

The Wild Hunt begins when the wind shakes the shingles and rattles the window; that is Odin riding his eight legged horse, Sleipnir, as he leads his great host through the country side. The roads and empty fields are no longer safe, for they aren't meant for the living; it is time for spirits, witches, and trolls. For this reason some people choose to celebrate this holiday on the same night as Halloween to more easily integrate their personal observances.

No matter the night you choose, this is a night to feast and to celebrate our connections with friends and family. It is a great time to reflect, to look back over the previous year and all that you accomplished. This is a night for bragging. Boast of your accomplishments, or those of a loved one, or a favored ancestor.

As you look back, make a toast as you remember those friends and family that have passed on. This is a festival that acknowledges and embraces the awe and respect that we have for death and the dead. Death is not an evil thing; we all live and therefore, we all die. That is why it is so important to remember. We all live on in the memory of our loved ones and in our deeds and accomplishments.

The divisions between the world of the living and the realms of the dead are diminished. The restless spirits of the dead and the yet to be born travel among the living. The dead return to the places where they once lived or to visit missed loved ones. Even if they aren't seen, you should raise a horn to honor their memories. They are the past that shaped our present as we shape the future for our descendents. Pay tribute to Odin, sacrifice to Freyja as you give thanks to your ancestors and venerate the deceased.

December/Yule 21 --Yule

The Winter Solstice is upon us. This is the beginning of twelve days of celebration and it is appropriately called Mother's Night. The celebrations are carried through the rest of the year ending on the Twelfth Night.

This is the midwinter celebration and without a doubt it is the most well known of the Heathen holidays. Many of its traditions, decorations, observations and terminology will be familiar, even if you're unfamiliar with the symbolism.

The tree itself represents Yggdrasil, the world tree and the colored balls hung from its limbs are symbolic of Idunna's golden apples. The tree itself used to remain outside, but when certain observances were outlawed, devout Heathens continued to celebrate by hiding the tree indoors. The wreath represents the sacred oath ring, perhaps the one that Odin sent with his slain son, Balder. The Yule Log is another old Heathen custom. The Yule Log was burned on the longest night of the year to remind everyone that life survives even in times of great darkness.

This holiday is all about the return of the sun and the warmer months to come. This season marks the return of the god Balder from the realm of the dead; once again he brings his glowing warmth back to the frozen earth. From this point on, the days will grow longer and the nights will shorten. The first night is Mothernight, when Frigga, the female ancestral spirits, and the living mothers are all honored. Mothernight represents the birth of the world from the darkness of winter. This is the shortest day of the year; therefore it is the longest night. It was traditional to stay up all night and make sure the sun was indeed going to rise again and bring her nourishing warmth. Currently, it may not be conceivable to hold an all night vigil, but you can rise early enough to greet her as she returns.

The celebration of Yule lasts for twelve days beginning at sunset on Mothernight, which is celebrated on the Winter Solstice. Because the solstice can fluctuate from year to year, my household has found it easier and more convenient to settle on one specific date to begin. We chose December 20th because we finish out the year in celebration of our gods and goddesses and begin a new year refreshed and invigorated.

Each one of the twelve days of Yule is a miniature reflection of the twelve months of the year. On the first night of Yule, you look back to what you accomplished last January and plan out what you intend for the upcoming January. The second day is for February, third for March, and so on until the twelfth night representing December.

On the twelfth night, we have Yule oaths that are sworn over a cup or horn of mead; now of course they are called New Year's Resolutions. You can boast your success of last year's oaths while you make new ones.

Yule is also the time when Odin's Wild Hunt becomes the most aggressive. It rides with maniacal speed and intentional recklessness, howling and cavorting as its time upon this plane of existence nears its end. It is a dangerous time to meet them, but if you leave out offerings of food and drink they will sometimes return the offering with blessings of fruitfulness.

Decorate an evergreen tree to remind yourself of Yggdrasil, the world tree. Hang symbols of Idunna's apples so you remember that spring is just around the corner. String white lights to remind you of the warmth of the sun and colored lights as a representation of those beautiful northern lights. Hang a wreath to celebrate the return of Balder, and the abundance that Draupnir, the oath ring, symbolizes. On the final night of Yule, it is customary to draw the rune Jera over your main entrance. It will bring you luck and good fortune over the next year.

During Yule, we celebrate Thor and his constant effort in battling the frost giants. We pay tribute to Frey and Freyja in the hopes of fertility and prosperity in the coming year. We honor Odin as the leader of the Wild Hunt, Chooser of the Slain, and Giver of Ancestral Wisdom. We thank Balder for his sacrifice and his beneficial return. We offer sacrifice to all of the Aesir and Vanir, gods and goddesses alike. The giving of gifts builds bonds and strengthens relationships. Our greatest creed is "a gift for a gift."

Afterward

You do not have to limit yourself to only honoring the gods that I put with each holiday. The great thing about being a Heathen is honoring your intuition. If you feel that a god or goddess should be honored during a particular part of the season, then do so. This is meant to be a guide not an absolute so definitely go with what you feel.

Marriage

The elements of marriage in literary sources are pretty scarce. We know marriage itself is sacred and important. But, the exact details of the ceremonies are lost. Some elements can be found hidden within Thrymkvida of the Poetic Edda.

Here is one example of a wedding ceremony.

The participants and spectators of the wedding are situated around the altar.

The groom's family and 2nd (Best Man) on one far side, and the bride's family and her 2nd (Maid of Honor) on the opposite side. The officiator (Gothi) is behind the altar in the center.

Best Man and Maid of Honor are to both walk to the center, stand before the Gothi.

Gothi: "Why have you come before our community and the gods?" Both Best Man & Maid of Honor: "We are here to see to the marriage of (groom's name) and (bride's name)."

Gothi says to Best Man: "Why should (bride's name) marry (groom's name)?"

Best Man answers of his own accord, speaking upon why he thinks groom is a good person, deeds groom has done or accomplishments ...etc.

Gothi says to Maid of Honor: "Why should groom's name marry bride's name?"

Maid of Honor answers of her own accord, speaking upon why she thinks the bride is a good person, deeds bride has done or accomplishments...etc.

Gothi says: "These are all good reasons, reasons enough for them to come forward to our community and our gods for their blessings. Bring them forward."

Best Man & Maid of Honor both walk back and bring bride and groom both in front of the altar.

Gothi says: "Are you both here to be married before the Aesir, the Vanir, and our community?"

Groom and Bride answer: "Yes."

Gothi says: "As our community and our gods & goddesses are important to us, so are our families. Do the families of (groom) and (bride) agree to this wedding?"

Families merely nod approval, or say simply, "Yes."

Gothi then picks up Miollnir representation, holds it high and says: "Mighty Thor, Warder of Midgard, we call upon you to bless this union with fertility & happiness. We ask you to protect & bless this new family!"

Gothi then waves hammer over the couple's heads.

Gothi then says: "Into Midgard we call upon Var and Sjofn, goddesses of oaths and love, we also ask you to witness these oaths in this union of marriage!"

Gothi picks up the horn and oath ring and says: "Know this: that this horn's tip falls into the Well of Wyrd, where your oaths will be sunk into eternity. Know this: that this oath ring lays your oaths and binds them together within you both. The Aesir, the Vanir and our community, await."

Groom and Bride take the horn and oath ring together.

Groom speaks his oath to Bride and drinks from the horn.

Bride speaks her oath to Groom and drinks from the horn.

They hand them back to the gothi.

Gothi pours leftover contents into the blot bowl.

Gothi asks for the rings. Both Maid of Honor and Best Man hand the gothi the rings.

Gothi holds the rings up and says: "Let these rings be a symbol of the oath and the love you both have for each other. A ring is forever in cycle and forever continuous, as should be your love for each other."

Gothi then hands Groom and Bride the rings.

Groom says: "(bride's name, my beloved, I give you this ring as a symbol of our love."

Bride says: "(groom's name), my beloved, I give you this ring as a symbol of our love."

They kiss.

Gothi says: "The Aesir and the Vanir, the gods and goddesses of our folk, and our community have borne witness to the oaths of this union. May your marriage be full of many blessings."

Gothi hands the blot bowl to Bride & Groom and they empty the bowl's contents into the bare ground.

]

Handfasting Ceremony

    Handfasting is another symbolic unity ritual in which a couple stands face to face as their hands are tied together – hence the phrase tying of the knot. As hands are bound, words are recited expressing love and commitment to each other.

    Traditionally two red cords are used during this ceremony. Red representing the blood each is willing to spill for the other if needed.

    A Bride and Groom can choose to bind one hand or two.

    For one hand, stand side by side and hold out arms together. For two hands, stand face to face and clasp each other by the hands or wrists. Couples can cross arms, with one left hand linking the others right, which looks like an infinity knot from above.

Knots are tied per preference of the bride and groom, from a simple knot to more elaborate wrapping of the wrists resulting in an impressive infinity knot. However, the knot is tied, the important part is that it should be so tight that you cannot pull it apart, symbolizing the strength of the marriage.

After the ceremony, hang the cords in the house as a reminder of commitment and forever strong ties.

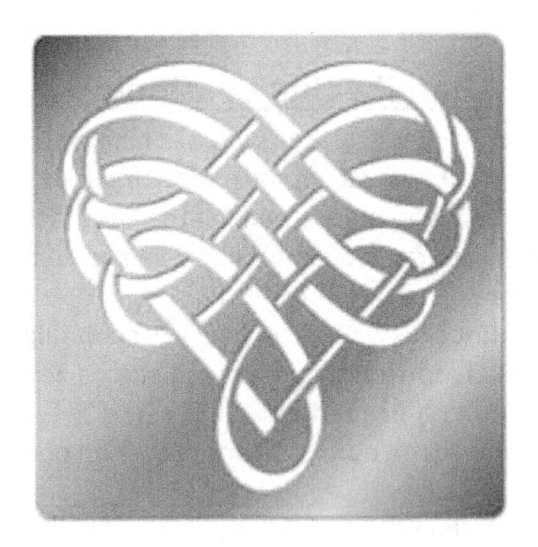

Blot

The blot is a mainstay of Heathen ritual and practice. It is a ceremony in which you honor the gods and goddesses while celebrating a particular holiday or event. A blot can be either a very formalized ritual or a very informal gathering. More formalized rituals are usually performed by a Heathen priest called a Gothi, or a priestess known as a Gythia.

The following is an outline of the steps that can be taken. They can be ritualized to a greater or lesser degree, depending on your needs and the needs of any other participants. A blot is technically a ritual that is conducted around a sacrifice. This traditionally takes place when you observe holidays but can also be designed for use when participating in other special events.

There are several steps; the first is called a consecration or hallowing. This is when you sanctify or make holy the place where the ritual will be performed by the Gothi or Gythia going to the four points of the compass carrying the ritualized version of Thor's hammer. They go to the Northern most point first and raise the hammer while standing in what is known as the Elhaz rune position. This is like a "Y", feet together and hands outstretched to the sky. The person who conducts the hallowing must loudly declare, "Hammer in the Northern Ways! Hallow and hold this holy stead!" They would then use the hammer to make the sign of the hammer in the air, that is an upside down "T". They then proceed to the East, South, and finally West, repeating the actions and the words used in the North. Replace the words, "Northern ways" accordingly.

The next step is to proceed back to the alter and invite the gods or goddess to attend the event. You are either honoring them or inviting them to witness an important event. That is where the next step comes in; it is where you give an explanation to the gathered worshippers or attendees of why you are performing the particular blot. For this you can get as creative or complex as your nature decides, or it can be very simple and basic. It can be a short statement of facts, a quote from a historical saga, or it can be a dramatic epic poem. The important part is to make sure that everyone understands what they are doing and who they are honoring.

The next step would be the physical act of making an offering or sacrifice. The sacrifice is an offering or gift that is made to one of the gods or goddesses. The gifts or offerings should always be kept in balance. A valued or valuable gift is offered in return for a gift that has already been bestowed upon you, and your sacrifice is a gift of gratitude. If you are offering a sacrifice before making a request then make sure that the sacrifice is of commensurate value for what you are about to ask the gods for. The cycle is always, a gift for a gift.

A form of sacrifice in the past was of course the ritual killing of an animal. The blood from the sacrificed animal would be captured in a ritual bowl known as either a Hlautbolli, or Blotbolli then be sprinkled over the altar and participants with a sprig of evergreen called hlautteinar. This is a ritualistic blessing that connects the gathered observers to the gods and goddesses along with the sacrifice and each other. The Gothi or Gythia would then hang up the head and hide of the animal while the meat would be consumed by worshippers in a celebratory feast.

We of course have to do things a little bit differently now days. We have to adapt to the morals of modern society, but we can still accomplish the same intended purpose by taking an alternate path.

Without the sacrifice of the animal we adopt mead as our intermediary. The Gothi or Gythia pours mead into a drinking horn, or vessel being used as such, and traces the sign of the hammer, an upside down "T", over the mead. The Gothi then holds the horn up to the sky as they ask the gods and goddesses to bless it and accept it as a sacrifice.

The mead having been blessed and sanctified is now used for toasting. The Gothi makes the first toast and then drinks. The horn is then passed to the next person, or it is handed to the assistant who carries it to each individual, the horn always travels in a clockwise direction. Each person lifts the horn up to the sky and makes a loud, robust, toast to the particular god or goddess being honored, then drinks.

This could incorporate a sumble which has three rounds of toasting, or it could be the single round. If it is the single round then after the final person toasts and drinks, the Gothi takes a final drink to finish the cycle then pours the remainder into the Hlautbolli. The evergreen sprig is dipped into the bolli and the mead is sprinkled across the altar.

The Gothi then proceeds in a clockwise direction; stopping in front of each participant and sprinkles them with the mead from the bolli, using the sprig of evergreen. The Gothi while sprinkling uses a "X" type motion. This is the symbol of the Gebo rune, which means gift.

After the sharing of the sacrifice and the giving of blessings, the remainder of the bolli is poured out in a specific place that has been set aside for this purpose. It is done to honor the landwights who may have gathered to watch. It may also be necessary to reassure them because the celebrating can become enthusiastic and even downright rowdy. Invocations and toasts to the gods and goddesses are often shouted because we want them to hear us all the way in Asgard.

Blots can be very simple and done in a short amount of time. This may be useful if there are time constraints or inclement weather. If weather is the issue then you can always do the blot quickly then move indoors to perform a sumble while feasting and entertaining.

A blot is usually a group affair but if you are a solo worshipper then it can always be modified. The most important thing to remember is that the blot is between you and the gods. If you need to make adjustments, then make them. Every aspect of Heathen religious observances can be modified to fit your personal needs and desires. These are only guides to help you find your path as you gain in knowledge and practice. Your skill and confidence will grow as you continue to practice.

After everything is wrapped up to your satisfaction all that remains is the ending. You can perform an elaborate closing or you can simply thank everyone for attending; gods, goddesses, landwights, and worshippers alike. A hail and farewell as you wish everyone safe travels as they wend their way home.

Sumble

A Sumble can be incorporated into a Blot or it can be performed separately with very little structure. At its most basic level a Sumble is several rounds of toast in which you remember or praise those who are worthy of being honored. It can take place at a wedding, a funeral, a holiday celebration or even a birthday party. You hold up the horn, make your toast loudly, and then drink deeply.

A Sumble will always consist of three rounds. The first round is to a god or goddess of your choosing unless it is being performed in a blot that is dedicated to a specific entity, then the first round is for them. The second round is when you would pay tribute to heroes, or to a deceased loved one. The heroes can be your personal heroes or they can be heathen heroes that inspire us all. Remember to speak loudly and boldly. If they are in the next world you want to make sure that they hear your words clearly. The third round is completely open to whatever you want. You can boast of your deeds or you can honor someone else's achievements. You can swear an oath or you can toast a loved one and what they mean to you. It is your choice.

If you or other participants can't or don't drink alcohol, then modify it. Everything can be modified to fit your personal tastes or group needs. In this case you can replace the mead with some form of juice; especially if the younger heathens are wanting to participate.

Not all Sumbles need to stick to the rounds that were listed earlier, although it is the more common structure. Another example is a Sumble that honors the Norns in a personal way. The first round would be to Urd and a specific event in your past that made you who you are today. The second toast would be for Verdandi and a situation that is currently taking place. The third round would be for Skuld and something that is to occur in the near future.

WARNING

It is not uncommon for Sumbles to turn into drinking contests. Heathens are a competitive lot and all who host one of these particular adventures should be cautious. Good luck to those brave and hearty hosts, and glory to the Heathen heart that remains standing at the end.

Lo Do I Behold

"Lo, there do I see my father.
Lo, there do I see my mother,
and my sisters, and my brothers.
Lo, there do I see the line of my people,
Back to the beginning!

Lo, they do call to me.
They bid me take my place among them,
In the halls of Valhalla!
Where the brave may live forever!"

RAGNAR'S DEATH SONG

It gladdens me to know that Balder's father makes ready the benches for a banquet. Soon we shall be drinking ale from the curved horns. The champion who comes into Odin's dwelling does not lament his death. I shall not enter his hall with words of fear upon my lips.

The Aesir will welcome me. Death comes without lamenting.

Eager am I to depart. The Disir summon me home, those whom Odin sends for me from the halls of the Lord of Hosts. Gladly shall I drink ale in the high-seat with the Aesir. The days of my life are ended. I laugh as I die.

Viking Funeral

Around 921 AD an Arab by the name of Ibn Fadlan came across a group of Vikings called the Rus. He was around them long enough to have witnessed a funeral, and we are lucky enough to have the details that he preserved. This is a small snippet of the manuscript that he wrote.
"I had heard that at the deaths of their great chiefs they did many interesting things, of which the least was cremation, and I was interested to learn more. At last I was told of the death of one of their outstanding men. They placed him in a grave and put a roof over it for ten days while they cut and sewed garments for him.
If the deceased is a poor man, they make a little boat, which they lay him in and burn If he is wealthy, they

collect his goods and divide them into three parts: one for his family, another to pay for his clothing and a third for the making of beer, which they drink until the day when his female slave will kill herself and be burned with her master. They stupefy themselves by drinking this beer night and day; sometimes one of them will die with his cup in his hand.

    When the man of whom I have spoken died, his girl slaves were asked, "Who will die with him?"

    One stepped forward and answered, "I."

    She was then put into the care of two young women, who watched over her and accompanied her everywhere, to the point where they occasionally washed her feet with their own hands.

    Garments were being made for the deceased and all else was being readied of which he had need. Meanwhile the slave drinks every day and sings, giving herself over to pleasure.

    When the day finally arrived for the deceased man and the girl to be cremated, I went down to the river where his ship sat. It was no longer in the water because they pulled it up onto the shore and secured it in an upright position by erecting four posts around the ship.

    While I stood staring at the ship on the shore, people began to approach the man where he still lay in the ground. They spoke words that I didn't understand, and then they would turn and walk away.

    By the afternoon of that tenth day, they had built a wooden pavilion in the middle of the deck of the ship. They covered this with various sorts of fabric and then placed a couch inside the pavilion. An old woman then came along and climbed onto the deck of the ship. My interpreter told me that she was the Angel of Death. She was the one in charge of having the clothes made and arranging all the other aspects having to do with the death. When I was told that she'd be the one to kill the slave girl, I gave the rotund old woman a second look.

My attention didn't linger long though as my eyes were drawn to the activity at the grave. A group of men removed the wooden roof they'd erected and then lifted out the dead man who was still clad in the garments he had died in. His body had been turned black by the frigid temperature of the land. They removed some intoxicating drink, fruit and a stringed instrument that I hadn't realized they'd put in with him. They removed the body, the drink and the instrument. Surprisingly the dead man did not smell bad, only his color had changed.

They removed his old clothes and dressed him in trousers, stockings, boots, a tunic and caftan of brocade with gold buttons. They gave him a fur hat and then carried him into the pavilion on the ship. Once they had the chief sitting on the couch in an upright position, they brought his weapons and placed them by his side. Next they brought out the deceased's two favorite horses and ran them around until they were covered in sweat. Then, they whipped out their swords and cut the horses into pieces before throwing them onto the ship. Next, they slaughtered a rooster and a hen before throwing their remains onto the deck of the ship.

After this, the lead men seemed to retire to nearby tents that had been arranged in a half circle. When I observed the slave girl leaving one tent and going into the next, I asked my interpreter, "Why is she visiting each of those men?"

He replied, "She is having sexual intercourse with each man so that he can send a message of love with her."

She spent all day pursuing this endeavor until late in the afternoon. They then led her to a spot where they had erected what resembled a door frame. Several of the men that she had recently visited bent over with their arms interlaced, and she stepped up onto the platform of their arms. They raised her up so she could look over the top of the door frame. She then spoke.

I looked to my interpreter for a translation.

"She said, 'Behold, I see my father and mother.'"

They then raised her up a second time and he interpreted without my prompting. "I see all my dead relatives seated."

She was raised a third time. "I see my master seated in Paradise and Paradise is beautiful and green; with him are men and boy servants. He calls to me. Take me to him."

They lowered her to the ground and the crowd followed as she was escorted to the ship. She stopped in front of the old woman known as the Angel of Death. She took off the two bracelets that she was wearing and handed them to the old woman. She then proceeded to remove the only two rings she was wearing and handed them to the two girls who had served her. That was when I was informed that they were the daughters of the Angel of Death.

The same men who had lifted her to look over the door frame moved in and lifted her up onto the deck of the ship. She stood silently and looked at the pavilion that covered her master, but she wasn't immediately made to enter.

A large group of men neared the ship; each one carried a shield and a large stick. No one took this to be out of the ordinary so I focused my attention back on the girl.

She was handed a cup of some intoxicating drink where as she sang before drinking it down in one motion. My interpreter informed me that she was bidding farewell to all her female companions.

She was handed a second cup and she began to sing again. This song seemed to drag on for longer than normal because the old woman began gesturing for her to drink. She finally gulped it down, and within moments seemed to lose focus. The old woman gestured toward the pavilion and the girl started to move in the direction, but then grew distracted and stumbled.

The old woman seized her by the head and forcefully escorted her into the pavilion. That's when the group of men with the shields began to bang their sticks on the shields. The noise was so loud that I was forced to lean my head close to the interpreter so he could enlighten me as to what was happening.

"They are making sure that if she cries out that the other slave girls do not hear her. It wouldn't do for her screams to scare off any potential volunteers for when their masters die."

I then watched as six men climbed on board the ship and entered the pavilion. I again looked to the interpreter. "They are also sending messages of love to her master."

The Angel of Death had emerged from the pavilion, and like the rest of us, she waited. It took quite a while but eventually one side of the entrance of the pavilion was pulled aside. One end of a looped cord slipped from the sleeve of the old woman's garment as she went back into the pavilion.

There was nothing but silence so I relied upon the interpreter once again.

"The slave girl will be stretched out. Two of the men will hold her feet while two others will hold her arms. The two strongest will be given the ends of the cord. They loop it around her neck and while they strangle her, the Angel of Death will stab her to death. They will then place her next to her master."

The events he described didn't take much longer to occur than the telling did. Within moments of him growing silent, the six men and the Angel of Death emerged from inside the pavilion and climbed down from the ship. The old woman was decorated with splatters of blood and without pause, made her way through the crowd and out of sight.

People began piling wood, limbs, and other debris beneath and around the ship. Then relatives of the dead man approached with torches lit from a nearby fire. They lit the wood beneath the ship and then stepped back. After a short while other people began to light their torches and depositing them on and around the ship.

The flames began to engulf the wood, the ship, and finally the pavilion. A strong wind arose and began to blow at the flames. The fire grew quickly and became so fierce that the intensity caused everyone to step back.

One of the Rus looked directly at me and made a comment. I asked the interpreter what he had said.

"He said, 'You Arabs are fools.'"

"Why?" I asked.

He said, "You take the people who are most dear to you and whom you honor most and put them into the ground where insects and worms devour them. We burn him in a moment, so that he enters Paradise at once." Then he began to laugh uproariously.

"Why do you laugh?" I asked.

"Because his Lord, for the love of him, has sent the wind to bring him away in an hour."

And it came to pass that after only an hour, the ship, the wood, the girl and her master were nothing but cinder and ash.

In other research, and in more modern times, during the ceremony poetry may be read to remind the loved ones of the beginning of a new life for the one who has passed. A loved and favorite poem I have found for this is "Do Not Weep For Me".

Do not weep for me for I have not gone. I am the wind that shakes the mighty Oak. I am the gentle rain that falls upon your face. I am the spring flower that pushes through the dark earth. I am the chuckling laughter of the mountain stream.

Do not weep for me for I have not gone. I am the memory that dwells in the heart of those that knew me. I am the shadow that dances on the edge of your vision. I am the wild goose that flies south at Autumns call and I shall return at Summer rising. I am the stag on the wild hills way. I am just around the corner.

Therefore, the wise weep not. But rejoice at the transformation of my Being.

Realms of the Dead

Heathen conceptions of an afterlife are varied and complex. The existence of a Self is a given, but what happens to it at death can take several paths.

There is no judgment by the gods when it comes to the Self's final destination. You determine your ultimate fate. It is a determination that is created by your Wyrd and by your ability to adapt to the Orlog and Hamingja that you may have inherited. Of course your final destination may also be determined by the circumstances of your death, the particular god or goddess that you most identify with, or even your personal desires. In other words, there can be al lot of variables. A Heathen afterlife and its consideration is not as simple and straight forward as other belief systems. As an individual though, it may be very straight forward for you. You may be absolutely convinced and sure of where your Self will go. If that is the case, then embrace it and do not let anyone sway you from that belief.

For those who are not aware of the possibilities or are unsure of their final destination; here are the realms of the dead that a Heathen may look for.

The most familiar and most documented realm is of course Valhalla. This is the hall where warriors dedicated to Odin longed to be. Whenever a battle was on the verge of taking place, it was Odin who sent out the Valkyries to select the slain warriors. The Valkyries rode out on steeds that were so fleet of hoof that they could travel through the skies. Warriors fought valiantly in search of these noble deaths in battle. It was their sincere desire to see a Valkyrie swooping down to collect them at the moment of their death; to carry them to Valhalla as one of Odin's chosen.

Valhalla means "hall of the slain," and it has five hundred and forty doors that are all wide enough to allow eight hundred warriors to walk out side by side. Above the main gate is mounted a boar's head, and perched on the top of it is an eagle with an all encompassing gaze.

The walls of the great hall are fashioned from golden spears that have been polished to such a high gloss that they light up every corner of every room. The roof is made up of overlapping golden shields, and the benches are covered by the finest armor. Long tables line the room with enough seating to accommodate every Einherjar.

Bragi, the god of eloquence and poetry greets all newcomers with a horn of mead and a recitation of all their great deeds. When a special favorite of the one eyed god is brought into Asgard; Odin becomes Valfather, father of the slain. He rises from his golden throne and personally greets the warrior as he enters into Valhalla.

The Valkyries, choosers of the slain, discard their battle armor when they aren't engaged in searching battlefields. They don feminine white robes and pass out horns of mead and slabs of boar's meat.

The meat given to the Einherjar is from the flesh of the divine boar Saehrimnir, a fantastic creature that regenerates itself daily. Once it regenerates, it is slain by

Valhalla's cook Andhrimnir, and then cooked in the great cauldron Eldhrimnir.

The mead they drink flows freely and constantly from the udders of the goat Heidrun. This she-goat only eats the tender leaves and twigs from the top branches Yggdrasil.

Once the warriors have eaten and drank their fill they rush out into a vast, open courtyard. There they duel and battle; fighting against one another to improve their skills in battle. No matter the grievous wounds or serious injuries they inflict upon one another; they are all healed when the dinner horn is sounded.

They spend their days in battle and their nights in pleasure as they await the call of Heimdall's horn. This will be the signal for them to join the gods and fight against the giants in the final battle known as Ragnarok.

Another destination for the fallen warrior could be the field of the people, or better known as Freyja's hall: Folkvang. Freyja is most often thought of as goddess of beauty and sexual desire, but there are other aspects to her nature. She is the goddess of the magic known as Seidr, and this is the very magic that she taught to Odin. For teaching him this magic he gave her the first choice of the chosen slain.

This may have been what made her queen of the Valkyries, and in this guise she is called Valfreyja. It is said that she leads the Valkyries down to the battlefields ensuring that she gets first claim. She then transports her chosen ones to Folkvang where they are richly rewarded.

Freyja's hall is also the destination for all of those who practice magic, and those who are especially dedicated to her. Along with Fensalir, Folkvang also welcomes wives and their husbands, but Freyja's hall Is not exclusive to just married couples. Any lovers who are sufficiently dedicated to one another can reap the rewards of her hospitality.

The joys of her dwelling are so enticing that some women would rush into battle if they saw their loved one slain just to join him there. Others would commit suicide once they heard of their lover's death in order to join them that much sooner. The traditional method for this was with a sword or knife. The more extravagant way was for the woman to throw herself on the funeral pyre of her lover so that she'd be immediately transported to him.

The next realm of possibility for the deceased could be the Marsh Halls. This is Fensalir and it belongs to the queen of Asgard, Odin's wife, Frigga. This is where the goddess invites those husbands and wives that are deeply in love and so dedicated to one another that they never want to be separated. Fensalir is where they can go and enjoy each other's company forever. Frigga, who is the goddess of conjugal and motherly love has a genuine tenderness for married lovers and tender parents. That's why she has also opened her home to those children who are never born, and the ones who were too young to have developed a Wyrd of their own.

Within Fensalir, the goddess Gefjon has an entire wing of the palace. This is where she invites all the young ladies who never married, a place where they can live happily forever. I'm assuming that Frigga may recruit them for light babysitting duties from time to time.

Next, we have Ran, who is the goddess of death for all who perish at sea. With her husband Aegir, she has nine daughters who are wave maidens. Waves who are temperamental by nature, and at their worst they stir up the seas and assist their mother as she goes after doomed sailors. Ran has a giant net that she uses to capture her prey, which she then drags down to her coral palace.

For those who love the sea; this would be the perfect afterlife. They get to sail the seas for as long as they desire, eat as much seafood as they can handle, and let's not leave out that Aegir is considered the finest brewer of ale in all the realms.

Ran is said to have a particular affinity for gold, and uses it to light up her darkened halls. So if you plan on sailing or going on a sea voyage, it may be a good idea to carry a few pieces of gold. You may receive a warmer welcome than expected if you happen to be invited into her particular realms.

The next realm of the dead is presided over by the goddess Hel. There are a lot of descriptions out there of this particular realm. Some call her palace Misery, the dish that she supposedly serves is called Hunger. They even named her maid, Sloth and her bed is called Sorrow. Most, if not all, these negative connotations were influenced by writers who had been indoctrinated into a new religion. The truth Heathen belief system never saw Hel as a place of despair and punishment. It was, and is, a place for those who die of old age, sickness and other common maladies. It is a place of rest and peace.

There are several different thoughts of what Hel is like and they could all be right, or be wrong. Some think it will be similar to Earth; a place where we continue to carry out our lives in a way of our choosing. It may be a step back to where small villages and more simpler times existed. A space for us to enjoy our family in a way that hectic lifestyles didn't allow. Others believe that it is a grey nothingness where we await a new birth. A place of calm before the Norns pluck us back out and insert us into a new life. This is of course the concept of reincarnation, which is a very common theme amongst our Heathen belief system. It is believed that you can only be reborn into your own family lines. If you are beloved and one of your descendants names a child after you, it increases the odds of your Self being reincarnated into that child. There is a reason why some names are repeated over and over, generation after generation within the same family line. Obviously the people who carried the name displayed such great characteristics that the family hoped each successive naming would embody them as well, and perhaps they truly did.

Think about the consequences of a name as you await the birth of your child. But just because it increased the likelihood of luring a particular individual, it is not a prerequisite. No matter what name someone carries, it is likely that a distant or near ancestor will be reincarnated within your family.

Another realm of the dead may be the funeral mound. Unlikely in our modern era with the restrictions upon burial customs, but still a possibility if you have the option. In the past a loved one would be buried on the family land with possessions to be used in the afterlife, a mound would then be erected over it. Offerings of food, drink, and other sacrifices would be made on a regular basis and an aspect of the individual would remain close to the family. Today it is very difficult to keep our loved ones close like that, but there are possibilities.

The spirit or Self may return to the land that they loved, or they may choose to return and watch over their family line. They could become what are called landwights; this is especially possible when the land has been passed down from generation to generation.

Along the same line of possibilities are the Disir. In several sources the Disir are explicitly called dead women, or the souls of dead women. Several Eddic sources lead to the conclusion that the Disir are some kind of female ancestral guardians. They are often seen in dreams as they hand out warnings or impart some form of knowledge to their descendants. In some instances they are seen around the house or property and are called landdisir.

The Disir are always a representation of a female spirit, and hence this particular destination may only be possible for someone with a strong, innate, motherly instinct or desire. It is possible that a returned male will become a landwight or housewight whereas a returned female's entity will become a landdisir, or simply a Disir. There may be a sexual distinction, but it could just as easily be someone's perception.

Of course with all aspects of heathenism there is a strong influence of the individual and the way that they believe and worship. For example if someone pays more tributes to Uller and they feel a strong connection to the loner god, then they could end up skiing and hunting through the forests of Yewdale. Or maybe, someone feels the pull of Frey and dedicate themselves to him, they may be destined for his hall in Alfheim.

Then we have Thor, the wielder of the mighty hammer himself, and his hall Bilskirnir. During the Viking era, Thor was the more popular god. Odin was seen as a god for royalty, berserkers, and those who sought out that noble death in battle. Not everyone seeks out that special spot in Valhalla, some fight to live but also face death without fear. The hammer that Heathens wear is a symbol of their faith, but is also a talisman of protection; Thor is viewed in the same way. Some found, and some still feel that Odin is a fickle god with a complex plan. Where Thor is seen as a reliable, honest, and trustworthy god. He is seen as a god for the common man, and hence Bilskirnir is the destination for the more down to earth Heathen.

Servants and thralls are welcomed into the largest hall in Asgard, all thought of elitism and subjugation are abandoned at the doors of Bilskirnir.

The fact is that the sources do not point to one all inclusive destination. If it did, then it would negate and ignore the very individuality that our ancestors proclaimed and that we continue to strive to embody. Each choice we make effects our future and changes our very existence, and if they are truly part of a concept as deep and profound as the Well of Wyrd, then they must also affect our final destination. The Self cannot be destroyed and there is a place for it. Whether you are destined for one of the great halls, reincarnation, or even an existence of calm and peace within Hel, the Self lives on.

Abridged Dictionary

For a more an expanded and comprehensive version, see Dictionary for The Modern Heathen by W. S. Hurst. Available on Amazon or through www.HeathenInc.net

Aegir - (uh-jeer) "Sea" – God of the sea, and husband of Ran. Together, they have nine wave daughters who are the mothers of Heimdall.

Aesir - (uh-seer) "Gods" – One of two different groups of Norse gods. The Aesir is comprised of Odin and most of the gods in Asgard. The other group is known as the Vanir.

Afi – (ah-fee) – "Grandfather" – Together with his wife Amma, they are the second couple visited by Heimdall when he was disguised as Rig.

Ai – (ah-ee) – "Great-Grandfather" – Together with his wife Edda, they are the first couple visited by Heimdall when he was disguised as Rig.

Alfheim - (alf-huym) "Elf Home" – The world of the light elves and those related to them. This realm was given to Frey as a tooth gift and he has ruled over it ever since.

Alsvider – (ouls-vihd-er) – "All Swift" – The horse that pulls the moon across the sky.

Alsvin - (ouls-vehn) "All swift" – One of the two horses that pull the sun across the sky.

Alvis - (oul-vihs) "All Wise" – The dwarf who engages in a battle of wits with Thor in order to win the ability to wed Thor's daughter Thrud.

Amma – (am-muh) – "Grandmother" – Together with her husband, Afi, they are the second couple visited by Heimdall when he was disguised as Rig.

Arvak - (ahr-vak) "Early Riser" – One of the two horses who pull the sun across the sky.

Asgard - (az-gahrd) "Aesir Enclosure" – The realm which contains the dwellings of the Aesir, and a few Vanir, including, but not limited to: Valhalla, Fensalir, Bilskirnir, etc.

Ask - (ask) "Ash Tree" – The first man. He was created from a piece of driftwood, right alongside the first woman, Embla.

B

Balder - (bahl-der) – The god of light, innocence and the new spring. Son of Odin and Frigga; married to Nanna, and the father of Forseti.

Barri - (bahr-ree) "Barley Island" – The grove where Frey and Gerda meet to consummate their love.

Bifrost - (buy-frahst) - "Shimmering Path" – The rainbow bridge that the gods use to travel between worlds. In modern society, where our beloved pets go to after death and wait for us to join in the next life.

Bilskirnir - (bihl-skihr-neer) - "Lightning Crack" – Thor's mighty hall; located in an area of Asgard called Thrudvang.

Bragi – (brag-ee) – "Foremost" – The god of poetry and eloquence. Noted for his wisdom and skill with words. Married to Idunna.

Breidablik – (bruy-duh-blihk) - "Broad Gleam" – Balder's residence.

Brisingamen - (brih-sihng-uh-men) – "Flaming Necklace" – Freyja's prized necklace that she obtained by spending a different night with each of four dwarfs.

Buri – (bur-ee) – "Father" – The giant that was licked from the salty blocks of ice by the primeval cow, Audhumla.

D

Dag – (dag) – "Day" – The son of Dellinger & Nott. Personification of day.

Draupnir – (drop-neer) – "The Dripper" – Odin's golden arm ring which drips eight rings of equal size and weight every ninth night.

E

Edda – (ed-duh) – "Great-Grandmother" – Together with her husband, Ai, they are the first couple visited by Heimdall when he was disguised as Rig.

Einherjar – (uyn-hahr-yahr) – "Lone Fighters" – The warriors who are slain in battle then taken to Valhalla by the Valkyries.

Embla – (em-bluh) – "Elm" – The first woman. Created by the gods alongside the first man, Ask. They were carved from two pieces of driftwood that were found on a rocky beach.

F

Fadir – (fah-der) – "Father" – Together with his wife Modir, they are the third couple visited by Heimdall when he was disguised as Rig.

Fenris - (fihn -rihss) – "Fen Dweller" – One of the three children Loki fathered with the giantess, Angurboda. The other two are Hel and Iormungandr. Fenris is the wolf who bit off Tyr's hand when the gods used a magical chain to bind him.

Fensalir – (fihn-suh-leer) – "Fen-Halls" – The dwelling place of the goddess Frigga.

Fiorgynn – (fee-or-gehn) – "Earth" – Fertility goddess and one of the names given for Thor's mother.

Folkvang – (fohlk-vayng) – "Field of the People" – The place where Freyja's hall, Sessrumnir, sits.

Forseti – (for-seht-ee) – "Chairman" – The god of legal justice and judicial proceedings. The son of Balder and Nanna.

Freki – (freh-kee) – "Gluttonous" – One of Odin's two wolves.

Frey – (fray) – "Lord" – The god of fruitfulness, peace and prosperity. The son of Niord and Nerthus, brother of Freyja and ruler of Alfheim.

Freyja – (fray-yuh) – "Lady" – The goddess of beauty, sexual desire and magic. The daughter of Niord and Nerthus, sister of Frey and Queen of the Valkyries.

Frigga – (frihg-guh) – The goddess of the sky, marriage and motherhood. Queen of Asgard, married to Odin and Balder's mother.

G

Garm – (gahrm) – "Rag" – The dog chained up just outside of Hel's realm.

Gerda – (gur-duh) – "Enclosure" – The daughter of Gymir and Angurboda. Married to Frey.

Geri – (gehr-ee) – "Greedy" – One of Odin's two wolves.

Giallarhorn – (gee-ahl-lahr-horn) – "Screaming Horn" – The horn that Heimdall will blow when Ragnarok begins.

Ginnungagap – (gih-nun-guh-gap) – "Beguiling Void" – The great abyss that existed between Niflheim and Muspellsheim before time began.

Gioll – (gee-ahll) – "Scream" – The river that marks the boundary of Niflheim.

Gladsheim – (glads-huym) – "Bright-Home" – The hall where the Aesir have twelve thrones.

Glitnir – (gliht-neer) – "Shining One" – The silver covered residence of Forseti.

Gna – (guh-nah) – Frigga's messenger. She can travel through the air, over land and sea, and is considered the representation of a refreshing breeze. She sees all that happens on earth and reports it back to Frigga.

Gnipa – (guh-nee-puh) – "Overhanging Ledge" – The cave in Niflheim where the hound, Garm, is chained up.

Grid – (grihd) – "Greed" – The mother of Vidar, with Odin.

Gulltop – (gooll-top) – "Golden Top" – Heimdall's horse.

Gullfaxi – (gooll-faksee) – "Golden Mane" – The horse ridden by the giant Hrungnir when he challenges Odin and Sleipnir to a race.

Gullinbursti – (gool-lihn-buhr-stee) – "Golden Bristles" – The golden boar created by the dwarfs and given to Frey.

Gullinkambi – (gool-lihn-kam-bee) – "Golden combed" – The Midgard rooster.

Gungnir – (goong-neer) – "Swaying One" – The spear that was made by the dwarfs and then given to Odin. Once it is thrown, it never misses its mark.

H

Habrok – (hah-brahk) – "High Breeches" – Named by Odin as the best of the hawks.

Hati – (hah-tee) – The wolf that pursues and will eventually swallow Mani, the moon.

Heidrun – (huy-droon) – The goat that stands on the roof of Valhalla and provides the Einherjar with mead from her udders.

Heimdall – (huym-dahl) – "World Brightener" – The watchman of the gods. He will blow his mighty horn, Giallarhorn, to warn the gods when Ragnork begins.

Hel - (hehl) – The daughter of Loki and Angurboda, and the sister to Fenris the wolf and Iormungandr. The goddess who presides over the dead who choose to make it to her realm.

Helheim – (hehl-huym) – "Hel's Home" – The realm of the goddess of the dead and the place where some go to await reincarnation, or the place for those who die of old age or sickness.

Hermod – (her-mahd) – "War-Spirit" – One of Odin's sons and the messenger of the gods.

Hildisvin – (hihld-ees-vihn) – "Battle Boar" – The boar that belongs to Freyja.

Himinbiorg – (hihm-ihn-bee-org) – "Heavenly Protector – The place where the rainbow bridge connects to Asgard and Heimdall's palace.

Hlidskialf – (lihd-skee-oulf) – "Gate Tower" – The throne that Odin sits on when he wants to look into the different realms.

Hodur – (hoh-door) – "Warrior" – The god of darkness and blind chance. The blind son of Odin who is tricked, by Loki, into killing his brother, Balder, with a dart made out of mistletoe.

Hoenir – (hoh-neer) – A travelling companion of Odin's. He gave motion and senses to mankind when he helped to create Ask and Embla.

Hraesvelgr – (Hrayes-vehl-ger) – "Corpse Swallower" – A giant eagle who sits at the northern most reaches and when he flaps his wings he produces the cold winter winds.

Hrimfaxi - (huh-rihm-faks-ee) – "Frosty Mane" – The horse that draws the night across the sky.

Hrungnir – (huh-ruhng-neer) – "Brawler" – The giant who raced against Odin and then was killed in a duel with Thor.

Hugin – (hoo-gihn) – "Thought" – One of Odin's two ravens.

Hyndla – (huynd-luh) – A seeress that Freyja takes one of her worshippers to visit.

I

Idavold – (ee-duh- vahld) – "Splendor-Plain" – The meadow where the gods who survive Ragnarok meet and begin anew.

Idunna – (ee-doon-nuh) – "Rejuvenator" – The goddess of youth and spring. Guardian of the golden apples that the gods eat to maintain their youth, health and vigor. Married to Bragi.

Iormungandr – (yor-moon-gander) – "Mighty Wand" – One of the three children that Loki had with Angurboda. He is also known as the world serpent because he grew to such a massive length that he is curled around the earth, laying on the sea floor.

J

Jotunheim – (yoh-toon-huym) – "Giant home" – The realm of the giants.

L

Landvidi – (land-vee-dee) – The home of Vidar.

Lif – (leef) – "Life" – She is one of the two people who are meant to survive Ragnarok.

Lifthrasir – (leef-thray-seer) – "Lust for Life" – He is one of the two people who are meant to survive Ragnarok.

Loki – (Loh-kee) – The god of mischief, and the hearth fire. He is Odin's blood brother and the father of several children.

M

Magni - (mag-nee) – "Strong" – One of Thor's sons. He will survive Ragnarok and with his brother, Modi, they will take up their father's hammer, Miollnir.

Midgard – (mihd-gahrd) – "Middle Enclosure" – The realm of man, earth.

Mimir – (mee-meer) – "Wise" – After the war with the Vanir, Mimir was sent as a hostage but after making the Vanir unhappy he was beheaded. Odin preserved the disembodied head and now consults it for advice.

Miollnir – (mee-ohl-neer) – "Lightning" – The hammer that was created by the dwarfs and then given to Thor.

Modi – (moh-dee) – One of Thor's sons. He will survive Ragnarok and with his brother, Magni, they will take up their father's hammer, Miollnir.

Mundilfari – (moon-dihl-fahr-ee) – The father of the sun, Sol, and the moon, Mani.

Munin – (moo-nihn) – "Memory" – One of Odin's two ravens.

Muspellsheim – (moo-spells-huym) – "Home of Fire" – The home of the fire giants and the fiery region on one side of the primeval void known as Ginnungagap.

N

Nagilfar – (nag-ihl-fahr) – "Nail Ship" – The biggest of all ships and the one that will carry the giants into battle when Ragnarok begins.

Narve – (nahr-vuh) – "Narrow" – The son of Loki and Sigyn and the brother of Vali.

Nastrond – (nas-trahnd) – "Corpse-Strand" – A dark and bleak hall woven together with the spines of serpents. It has north facing doors and icy venom drips from the frozen rafters.

Nidhug – (need-hoog) – "Vicious Blow" – The serpent that gnaws on the roots of Yggdrasil.

Niflheim – (nihf-ehl-huym) – "Dark Home" – The realm of freezing mists and the home of the boiling spring, Hvergelmir. A realm that existed on the opposite side of the primeval void known as Ginnungagap, directly across from Muspellsheim.

Niord – (nee-ord) – The god of sea winds, coastal waters and commerce. The father of Frey and Freyja.

Norns – (norns) – Three women of vague lineage and unknown beginnings. Urd, Verdandi and Skuld determine the fate of each man and god alike. They represent Past, Present and Future.

O

Odin – (oh-dihn) – "Frenzy" – The god of wisdom, runes, battle and sacrifice. Heroic warriors who die in battle go to his hall, Valhalla.

R

Ragnarok – (rag-nuh- rahk) – "Twilight of the Gods" – The end of one cycle and the beginning of the next. A time when the giants will attack the gods in a last great battle that will consume many.

Ran – (ran) – "Plunder" – The wife of Aegir, mother of the waves and goddess of the deep.

Ratatosk – (rat-uh-tahsk) – "Drill Tooth" – The squirrel that runs up and down Yggdrasil. He carries hate filled messages back and forth between the eagle that lives in the highest branches and the Nidhug serpent that gnaws on the roots.

Rig – (rihg) – "King" – The name that Heimdall used when he travelled to Midgard and created the three different classes or stages of human kind.

Rinda – (rihn-duh) – The woman Odin seduced so that she would give birth to Balder's avenger, Vali.

S

Saga – (sah-guh) – "Seeress" – The goddess of history. Odin is said to visit her daily so they can exchange stories.

Seidr – (say-der) – "Magic" – A form of magic that Freyja taught Odin in exchange for the first choice of the slain warriors, making her queen of the Valkyries.

Sessrymnir – (sehss-rihm-neer) – "Seat-Room" – Freyja's hall and the destination for half of those slain in battle.

Sif – (sihf) – "Relative" – The goddess of harvest. Married to Thor and the mother of his two daughters, Thrud and Lorride. She is also the mother of Uller, but his father is unknown.

Sigyn – (see-gihn) – "Victorious Friend" – Loki's third wife, mother of Vali and Narve. When Loki is bound to a rock and a venomous serpent hung above his head, Sigyn protects him from the poison that drips from the serpent's fangs. When the bowl is full and she has to empty it, the poison hits him and Loki shakes in pain, which causes earthquakes.

Skadi – (shah-dee) – "Harm" – The goddess of winter and the hunt. The daughter of the giant Thiassi, who abducted Idunna.

Skidbladnir – (skihd-blad-neer) – The magical ship which was created by the dwarf Dvalin and given to Frey.

Skinfaxi – (skihn-faksee) – "Shining Mane" – One of the two horses which pull the sun across the sky.

Skirnir – (skihr-neer) – "Bright One" – Frey's servant and friend, and the one he relied on when he sought to win Gerda.

Skoll – (skahll) – "Treachery" – The wolf who chases after the sun, Sol.

Skuld - (skoold) – "Debt" – The Norn who is the embodiment of the future; the other two Norns are Urd and Verdandi.

Sleipnir – (sluyp-neer) – "Slippery" – Odin's eight legged horse and the child Loki had with the stallion, Svadilfari, while he was shaped shifted into a mare.

Surtr – (ser-ter) – "Black" – The fire giant that stands guard at the border of Muspellsheim.

Suttung – (soot-toong) – "Sup-Heavy" – The ower of the mead of poetry, after he took it from the two dwarfs who murdered his parents.

Svadilfare – (svah-dihl-fahree) – "Unlucky Traveler" – The stallion who helped the giant architect build the wall around Asgard, also the father of Odin's eight-legged horse, Sleipnir.

Svartalfaheim – (svahrt-alf-uh-huym) – "Home of the Black Elves" – The world of the black elves, otherwise known as dwarfs, this is the realm of their underground home.

Svasud – (svah-sood) – "Delightful" – The father of Sumr.

T

Thialfi – (thee-oulf-ee) – "Swift Elf" – The brother of Roskva and one of the two servants that Thor got from Egil after one of his goats was lamed.

Thok – (thahk) – "Thanks" – The giantess who refused to weep for the dead god Balder in order to get him released from Helheim.

Thor – (thor) – The god of thunder, lightning, storms and soldiers. The defender of Asgard and Midgard and the son of Odin.

Thrall – (thrahll) – A slave.

Thrudheim – (throod-huym) – "Power Home" – The realm where Thor's hall, Bilskirnir, stands.

Thrym – (thrihm) – "Crash" – The giant who stole Thor's hammer and demanded to marry Freyja in exchange for returning it.

Tyr – (teer) – "God" – The god of martial honor, courage, victory and sacrifice. He sacrificed his sword hand so the Aseir could chain up Fenris, the wolf.

U

Uller – (ool-ler) – The god of hunting, archery, skiing and single combat. His mother is Sif but his father is unknown.

Urd – (oord) – "Fate" – The Norn who is the embodiment of the past. The other two Norns are Skuld and Verdandi.

V

Vafthrudnir – (vaf-throod-neer) – "Mighty Weaver" – The wisest of giants and the one that Odin engages in a deadly battle of wits.

Valhalla – (vahl-hahl-luh) – "Hall of the Slain" – The mighty hall where Odin gathers those warriors who are slain in battle.

Vali – (val-ee) – Son of Odin and Rinda. The emblem of spring and the avenger of Balder.

Valkyries - (vahl-kihr-ees) – "Choosers of the Slain" – A group of female warrior figures that are led by Freyja but are attendants of Odin. They are the ones who collect the souls of the dead warriors and transport them to Valhalla.

Vanaheim – (van-uh-huym) – "Home of the Vanir" – The realm of the fertility gods known as Vanir.

Vanir – (van-eer) – The second known group of the gods. This group includes Niord, Nerthus, Frey, and many others. These deities are most often associated with nature and fertility.

Ve – (vay) – "Sacred Enclosure" – Son of the giant Bor and the brother of Odin and Vili.

Vidar – (vee-dahr) – "Wide Ruler" – The god of imperishable matter and the symbol of resurrection and renewal. The son of Odin and the giantess, Grid.

Vigrid – (vee-grihd) – "Battle Surge" – The plain where the final battle of Ragnarok will be fought.

Vili – (vee-lee) – "Will" – Son of the giant Bor and the brother of Odin and Ve.

Vindsual – (vihnd-soo-al) – "Wind Chill" – The father of Vetr, who is the personification of winter.

Y

Ydalir - (ee-dahl-ihr) – "Yew Dales" – Dwelling place of Uller.

Yggdrasil – (ihgg-druh-sihl) – "Terrible Steed" – The world tree and the place where Odin hanged himself as a sacrifice to himself in order to gain the wisdom of the runes.

Ymir – (ee-meer) – "Groaner" – The primordial giant Odin, Vili and Ve slew and then created Midgard from the various pieces of his body.

About the Authors

W. S. Hurst is a practicing heathen and dedicated Volva who follows the ways of her ancestors by incorporating the Nine Noble Virtues into her life on a daily basis. She is a Kansas Native who shares her love, friendship and loyalty with Kristoffer Alric Allison.

Kris Allison is a dedicated heathen who follows ancestral and family traditions while studying heathen lore and European history. Born and raised in Oklahoma, currently living in Kansas, sharing his love and life with W. S. Hurst.

Together they prove that the greatest illusion in this world is the illusion of separation.

Additional books authored by the two are available through Heathen Inc www.HeathenInc.net.

- Tales of Asgard, Volume 1
- Tales of Asgard Volume 2
- Modern Heathen On the Go: Edda
- Modern Heathen On the Go: Gods and Goddesses
- Modern Heathen On the Go: Celebrations
- Modern Heathen On the Go: The Havamal + Self Reflection
- Modern Heathen On the Go: The Havamal, Rede of Honor, The Nine Noble Virtues, Six Fold Goals, Five Further Thews
- Modern Heathen On the Go: Runes
- The Elder Futhark Runes - Reading, Understanding, Using and Self-Chronicle
- Norse Revelations, Motivations + Inspirations
- Dictionary for the Modern Heathen